JOSE SILVA'S
EVERYDAY ESP

USE YOUR MENTAL POWERS TO SUCCEED IN EVERY ASPECT OF YOUR LIFE

JOSE SILVA JR.
WITH ED BERND JR.

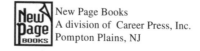
New Page Books
A division of Career Press, Inc.
Pompton Plains, NJ

JOSE SILVA'S EVERYDAY ESP
EDITED BY KRISTEN PARKES
TYPESET BY MICHAEL FRANCIS FITZGIBBON
Cover design by Scott Fray
Printed in the U.S.A.

To order this title, please call toll-free 1-800-CAREER-1 (NJ and Canada: 201-848-0310) to order using VISA or MasterCard, or for further information on books from Career Press.

The Career Press, Inc., 220 West Parkway, Unit 12
Pompton Plains, NJ 07444
www.careerpress.com
www.newpagebooks.com

Library of Congress Cataloging-in-Publication Data

Silva, Jose.
    Jose Silva's everyday ESP : use your mental powers to succeed in every aspect of your life / by Jose Silva Jr. with Ed Bernd Jr.
            p. cm.
    Includes bibliographical references and index.
    ISBN-13: 978-1-56414-951-0 (alk. paper)
    ISBN-10: 1-56414-951-X (alk. paper)
    1. Silva Mind Control. I. Berned, Ed, 1940- II. Title.
        BF1127.S54S55 2007
        133.8--dc22

                                                              2007024956

Dedicated to all humanity—all who were here before us, all those who are here now, and all who will come later—who are taking part in constructive and creative work to make the world a better place to live, so that when we move on, we shall have left behind a better world for those who follow.

ACKNOWLEDGMENTS

We want to thank Senior Acquisitions Editor Michael Pye for talking us into writing this book. It was a great idea, and we are glad you persuaded us to write.

We are grateful for Editorial Director Kristen Parkes' insights and questions that help make this a better book.

We appreciate how patient and understanding Editor Gina Talucci was as we made corrections and reworded some of the material to make sure we said what we wanted to say.

And a special thanks to Michael Fitzgibbon for adding the finishing touches and getting the book ready for you to read.

CONTENTS

Introduction

Are you a natural psychic but don't know it? Probably.

Have you ever thought of somebody, the phone rings, and it's that person? Or perhaps you say something at exactly the same time as a friend says or thinks it.

Have you ever dreamed of something, and then it happened the next day, or a few days later? Have you ever had a dream that contained information that helped you solve a problem? Most people have.

When you were younger, did you ever stare at somebody until they turned and looked at you? Or perhaps you knew you were being stared at even before you turned and looked at the person.

These are all examples of your own natural ESP at work.

You can easily develop your own ESP and learn to project your mind in order to detect information, which will help you make better decisions about health, relationships, business, personal development, and even your purpose in life.

BE MORE TIMES RIGHT THAN WRONG

Bad decisions lead to disappointment, unhappiness, suffering, and failure.

Good decisions bring you success, happiness, respect, fulfillment, and love.

Have you ever felt as if there was something more you should be doing with your life? Maybe you felt that there is a hidden talent just ready to burst into success, or a special mission, a soul purpose, you are ready to achieve?

Wouldn't it be nice to have guidance from higher intelligence as to how to achieve more? That's what Jose Silva's UltraMind ESP System is all about: To help you make the rest of your life the best of your life.

7

PRACTICAL ESP

Is there any practical value in ESP, or is it just for special occasions? Can it actually be useful in everyday life?

Absolutely. ESP (also known as intuition) can help you in every area of your life. There are countless examples of people using ESP in their everyday lives to help them regain and maintain outstanding health, fitness, and energy; build fulfilling and valuable relationships in their personal and business lives; and find and succeed in their life's work.

Everyday ESP was valuable to a lady named Catherine Ong from Australia, who was very uncomfortable having the surgery her physician had prescribed for a lump in her breast. On her way into the hospital, she ran into someone who arranged a consultation with another doctor, and, as a result, Catherine took a different approach that turned out to be exactly what she needed. You can read about how she was guided by coincidences in Chapter 10.

Doctors also find Everyday ESP valuable. In Chapter 10, you can read how intuition helps Dr. Calvin Poole detect problems long before lab tests confirm them. In Chapter 11, Dr. Clancy McKenzie explains how he uses information he receives in dreams to help him identify problems and find their solutions.

Katherine Handorf found great value in Everyday ESP: First it opened her eyes to a bad relationship she was in, then, when she least expected it, while doing a favor for a friend, Everyday ESP guided her to the man she is married to today. All the details are in Chapter 12.

Dolores, a lady who works in the high-tech industry in the northwestern United States, used Everyday ESP to get out of a bad job and into a better one. Su Irons from Australia took a different approach: she programmed to help her bad boss find another job. You can read their stories in Chapter 16.

There are many other examples of the benefits of Everyday ESP: In Chapter 10, Lang Ping of China tells how she was guided to a natural remedy for a painful menstrual period. Mme Xue Kuiyang, the first Silva UltraMind instructor in China, tells how her Everyday ESP may have found a problem on a commercial airplane before it took off.

In Chapter 16, you'll learn how Penny Atwell of Maine obtained help from higher intelligence to help her find the perfect buyer for her beloved historic old home, and how Tomoki Takahashi from Japan was guided to the perfect apartment.

In Chapter 6, you will learn a technique which my father developed shortly before his passing, which you can use to attract coincidences which will guide you to success in every area of your life: good health, fulfilling relationships, sufficient resources to meet the needs of you and your family and to fulfill your mission in life, and the guidance and insight that you need in order to do what you were sent here to do.

START USING YOUR ESP TODAY

There are three different ways you can learn to enter the powerful alpha brain-wave level and activate your mind in order to correct problems, overcome impediments, program yourself to achieve success, and to develop your natural God-given intuition. You will learn two of them in this book.

Next, I will teach you four of the most valuable ways to actually use your intuition in order to help yourself, help others, and communicate with a higher power—a power that we call higher intelligence—in order to learn your mission in life and to obtain the guidance and support you need to carry out your mission.

For example, in Chapter 6, we'll show you a scientific way to communicate with higher intelligence to help you make better decisions and fulfill your mission in life. In Chapter 7 we'll cover several aspects of psychometry, the art of detecting information by being near or touching an object, and how you can charge objects around the house with mental messages that can affect other people. Prof. John Mihalasky reports on the findings of his groundbreaking 10-year research project into the success of intuitive executives in Chapter 17. And finally, in Chapter 18, a psychiatrist explains how he used creative insights from the alpha level, along with coincidences from higher intelligence, to uncover the cause and treatment of depression and schizophrenia.

WHY ESP IS VALUABLE

Here are three of the reasons ESP is so valuable:

First, you can use your intuition to detect information that is not available to your physical senses. Why is that valuable? As my father always said, there is no such thing as a problem without a solution, only problems for which we do not have enough information to know what the solution is. Once you have enough information, it is easy to make a decision and solve the problem.

Second, you can project your mind—we call it Effective Sensory Projection—to correct problems mentally. This is exactly how distant healing, also called prayer healing, works. You can project a mental image of perfect health in order to attract matter to return to the perfect mold that the Creator provided for the physical body.

Third, you can use your ESP to communicate with higher intelligence in order to obtain guidance and support to make better decisions and fulfill your mission in life. My father used to refer to this as getting help "from an invisible means of support."

Once you know what needs to be done, you can use your mind to make the correction in the subjective dimension first. Everything begins in the mind; first you think a thing, then you do it. At the powerful alpha brain-wave level that we will discuss in Chapter 1, you can mentally correct any abnormality, then it will be easier to bring out the correction in the physical dimension also.

How you can develop your God-given ESP

In this book, I will provide you with two ways to learn—on your own—how to function at the correct level of mind where you can develop and use your Everyday ESP. The fastest way is to use the audio CD included with this book. If you prefer, you can practice on your own the way I will explained to you in the first two chapters. If you have already learned to function at the powerful alpha brain-wave level, then you can use the mental exercise on the CD and the countdown exercises in this book to reinforce and deepen your level.

You will need to invest a few minutes every day to learn to use the alpha brain-wave level. This small investment of time will pay big dividends because soon it will become automatic, and you will be using the alpha level to do your thinking without even realizing it. You will be detecting information with ESP just as easily and naturally as using your other senses.

We continue to help you even after you complete the book, because we want you to continue to use your Everyday ESP to correct problems, improve conditions on planet earth, and help convert the planet into a paradise.

In order to support and help you continue to practice and use your ESP every day of your life, we will provide you with access to a special private Website with more information and stories from other people just like you and how they use Everyday ESP to help them cope with the problems they encounter, to overcome those problems, and to move on to successful outcomes.

In order to benefit from your ESP, you need to use it every day. For the first few weeks, you will spend most of the time dedicated to Everyday ESP practicing and learning how it feels and how it works. After that it will take only a few minutes each day to actually use your Everyday ESP to bring about the results that you desire.

When you do this, you will be repaid many times over for the modest amount of time it takes to develop your Everyday ESP, as you are guided to solutions to problems, and to the resources that will help you do your job the best possible way.

JOIN THE SECOND PHASE OF HUMAN EVOLUTION ON THE PLANET

There is so much value to Jose Silva's Everyday ESP that millions of people around the world have used it during the last 40 years. Now we have a new tool, the MentalVideo, which is so powerful that it actually opens the door to what my father called "the second phase of human evolution on the planet."

When writing this book, we took the best material from *Jose Silva's UltraMind ESP System* (2000) and added new insights and experiences from graduates, as this new course and new way of thinking grows and spreads throughout the world.

Thank you for joining us on this mission, and congratulations on making the decision and doing what is necessary to fulfill your mission in life, so you will have the satisfaction of knowing that you have lived the successful life you were sent here to live, and have helped to make the world a better place to live.

As my father used to say, "May the rest of your life be the *best* of your life."

Section I: Welcome to The Silva Method

Chapter 1
Success Depends on How You Use Your Mind

Have you ever noticed that being born to wealth and privilege doesn't guarantee success in life, nor does growing up in poverty condemn one to failure?

Success doesn't depend on how much or how little formal education you have—it never has. Microsoft founder Bill Gates is a college dropout who just happened to become the wealthiest person in the world. Michael Dell was so busy building computers for other students that he had to drop out of the University of Texas, and today Dell is the biggest personal computer manufacturer in the world. Edison and Einstein were poor students, and Abraham Lincoln had little formal education.

My father had no formal education at all. While other 6-year-olds went to school, he went to work to support his family. His father was killed in an act of terrorism during the Mexican Revolution when he was just 4 years old, and his mother remarried and moved away. He certainly didn't get any special advantages when he was a child, yet he always seemed to be very lucky. He had a knack for making good decisions, and for doing the right thing at the right time.

He is not the only person who has a lot of good luck, of course. Other people have the habit of being at the right place at the right time and making the right decisions to bring them success.

SEEKING THE SECRET OF SUCCESS

How do they do it? My father began to wonder about that after he got married and his family began to grow. I was the first of his 10

15

children. By the time he had three children, he began to study psychology books to see if he could find the answer. He knew that his success didn't come from formal education or parental guidance, because he didn't have any.

Sigmund Freud didn't provide him with a direct answer, but guided him in a direction that yielded results. Freud had tried hypnosis, so my father got a book on hypnosis and tried it out on his children. He usually worked with my sisters and brothers while I observed. When I got a little older, I began to make audio recordings of all the sessions.

My father soon discovered that my siblings could do some pretty amazing things when they were at the correct level of mind. They would follow his instructions, including the instruction to remember the lessons he would read to them.

Even today, my brother Tony can still recite the poem "Invictus" more than 40 years after he learned it while in a hypnotic state.

But that's not all that happened under hypnosis. My sister Isabel began to guess what poems my father was going to ask her to recite back to him, and she guessed accurately. "It was like she was guessing my mind," my father explained later.

He thought that maybe they had worked together so much that she knew what to expect of him. To confirm that she didn't really have any "special powers," he asked her some questions that he didn't know the answers to, and to his surprise, when he checked out what she told him, he discovered that she had given him the correct answers.

The implications of that were enormous. He had invested a lot of time and effort in hypnotizing her, reading poems and lessons to her, and finding out what level she had to be at in order to recall them, and yet she could give him accurate answers about things she had never studied.

She could make stronger impressions of information on her brain neurons when she was at a certain hypnotic level, and then her mind could recall that information with the help of a post-hypnotic suggestion.

In addition, while at that same level, her mind also could detect information that was impressed on my father's brain neurons, and apparently information that had been impressed on other people's brain neurons, too.

Information is valuable in helping you succeed in life. If you have the right information, it is easy to make the correct decision. "There is no such thing as a problem without a solution," he used to tell us, "only problems for which you don't yet have enough information to know what the solution is."

He reasoned that Isabel's ability to detect "secret" information that was "hidden away" in other people's brains could be a wonderful "secret weapon" in all aspects of life.

He was so excited that he wrote to Dr. J.B. Rhine at Duke University and told him that he had trained his daughter to be a psychic. Dr. Rhine had conducted many years of research to prove that psychic ability was real, that some people had what he called an "extra sense." He even coined a term for it: Extra Sensory Perception, or ESP for short.

Dr. Rhine wrote back and told my father that it wasn't possible to train somebody to be a psychic, that only a few special people had the ability and others didn't. He told my father to be grateful that one of his children had that "special" ability, but not to fool himself into thinking that he had somehow taught it to her, because she had the ability all along.

My father was disappointed, and skeptical. After all, he had known Isabel all her life. He even helped deliver her. She had never displayed any psychic ability until he started hypnotizing her and taking her to different levels of mind. It was at these altered states of consciousness that she was able to detect information about things to which she had never been exposed.

What would it take to convince the scientist, Dr. J.B. Rhine, he wondered. He decided to take a scientific approach and pre-test his subjects to determine whether they had any psychic ability before taking them to the mental level where they could function as psychics.

"I didn't think that the Creator would discriminate," he said. "I didn't think that the Creator would give only a few people some special ability, and not give it to everyone else. I felt that we all had this special ability, and we just needed to be taught how to use it. I felt that it was like the ability to read, we all have the ability to learn to read and write, but most of us need to be taught."

He always believed that if anybody could do a thing, then everybody could learn to do that thing. He didn't believe that the Creator would give some few people some kind of "extra" ability that other people didn't have. Some might do it better than others, but he believed that if something can be done, then anybody can learn to do it.

My father was a good example of that. "My sister and brother taught me how to write my own name," he recalled, "so that I wouldn't have to make a little x, but could actually write my name." Once they got him started, he continued to learn on his own.

ONE COINCIDENCE THAT CHANGED MANY LIVES

That quest for knowledge is how he got into electronics repair. The year was 1928, just a few years after the first commercial radio stations went on the air. My father, who was 14 years old at the time, stopped by the barber shop one day to read some comic books. That is how he practiced his reading. The pictures in the comic books would help him understand the words that were written there.

On this day, there was a different kind of book. It was the first lesson in a correspondence course on radio repair. He began to read it, and it made sense to him. "It said that if you took a wire, no matter how long, and put an electron in one end, another electron would come out the other end," he recalled. "They compared it to a long tube filled with marbles. If you put a marble in one end, another marble will be forced out the other end."

The more knowledge you have, the more ways you have of earning money to support the family, so he asked the barber if he could borrow the book so he could study it.

"Oh, that is a valuable book," the barber answered. He offered to rent it to my father, who quickly agreed. My father had developed a business where he and other kids would sell merchandise door to door, and he was making good money at it, so he could afford to pay the barber and rent the book.

But then the barber added another condition: He wanted my father to take the tests, fill out the questions at the end of each lesson, sign the barber's name, and send them in.

That was fine with my father. He just wanted the information. So the barber got a nice diploma to hang on the wall of his barber shop, and my father used the knowledge he had gained to open a radio repair business that eventually became the biggest in South Texas.

While working with his children and studying psychology, he began to think about all of the coincidences in his life that had guided him to so much success. It wasn't just the information gained through study and through psychic ability that had led to success; there were coincidences that guided and helped him every step of the way.

One of the most significant coincidences came on a rainy Saturday morning after he had decided to end his research.

A SERIES OF COINCIDENCES

In 1949, after my father had been conducting research for about five years, he became so frustrated with his study of psychology that he decided to quit.

But something—or someone—wouldn't let him. As he recalled:

Freud, Adler, Jung—these intelligent, educated men—they cannot even agree with each other. How could I, a simple, uneducated man, ever hope to understand? If these bigwigs don't agree with each other, who am I to straighten them out? I am just an amateur!

At this time, I was working a very busy schedule. I closed my radio repair shop at 9 p.m. to go home to have dinner with my family. Late one night I sat in the living room reading a psychology book while my wife, Paula, and the children slept. But I'd had enough.

I've learned enough to help my family, I thought. *My church thinks I'm wrong to delve into these areas. People in the town, religious people, are beginning to shun me. I'm taking time and money that I could use for my family and spending it on this research. Why should I continue?*

I threw the book across the room. Paula heard it hit the wall after it slid under the sofa. Apparently someone on the other side did, too.

A message from higher intelligence

I went to sleep right after that, but two hours later a bright light inside my head woke me up. It was a light like the midday sun when you look up into space on a cloudless day. Hanging in space were two sets of numbers, one on top of the other. The first set was 3-4-3; the second set, under the first set, was 3-7-3. Right after that, an impression of Christ and *One Solitary Life* given to me at the army reception center came to me. *Why Christ?* I wondered. *Why me? What does this have to do with the numbers?*

I opened my eyes and it was dark. I glanced at the clock on the nightstand. It was 4:30 a.m. I said to myself, *Maybe it was a telepathic message.* I had become aware of parapsychology by this time, and had read that such things could happen. I figured maybe this was the way it was done.

Fascinated, I tried some experiments with myself and the light. I closed my eyes and tried to keep the bright light from disappearing, because it was fading gradually. I tried breathing slowly, but that did not help. I tried changing positions, but that did not help. I tried to slow down my heart, but whatever I did was not enough. The light faded until it disappeared.

I stayed awake the rest of the night, trying to analyze what had happened. I thought of Paula and how she used to tell me that people who read too much go crazy! I was not about to tell her about the light in my head because I knew her answer would be, "I told you so!" In fact, I might have agreed with her, as I started thinking, *Maybe this is how people start going crazy, by seeing lights in their heads.* But one thing I kept thinking was that, for whatever reason this happened, it must be all right because of the impression of Christ and *One Solitary Life* that came to me with the experience.

Searching for answers

The first explanation I thought of was that maybe I was supposed to call someone who has that phone number (a number including those specific sequences). I searched the telephone book from cover to cover but did not find any listing for the numbers.

My next idea was that maybe I should go to someone's home who had these numbers as part of their address, because maybe they would have a message for me. But when I studied a city map, I found that the home addresses in Laredo, Texas, did not use those numbers.

It was about four in the afternoon when I came up with another idea: I'd look at automobile and truck license plate numbers. I did this for the rest of the day, ready to ask for my message from the driver of any vehicle that had those numbers, but I did not find a car or truck license to match my mysterious numbers.

It was 15 minutes before 9:00 when I started to close my shop. My wife came in from our house next door and said to me, "If you go across the river into Nuevo Laredo, Mexico, for a service call, please get me a bottle of alcohol." (We use Mexican alcohol for medicinal purposes because it is pure and costs less than alcohol in Laredo.) I said to Paula, "Honey, I don't have service calls from across the border, but I will go and get you a bottle anyway."

A friend has another idea

At that very moment, an old friend of mine came in to invite me to go for some coffee. I said, "Help me to close my place and we'll go right now." I asked him if he was in a hurry or if we could take a ride to Mexico for Paula's alcohol.

Since my friend had been studying psychology with me for a year, I told him about my experience the night before. I felt sure he was not going to think I was crazy. I had not told anyone all day, and I needed to tell someone, so I told him. While crossing the bridge into Mexico, my friend suggested, "Now that we are coming into Mexico, and Mexico operates a national lottery, maybe there is such a number." I hadn't thought of that, and I had nothing to lose—the lottery agency was just a block and a half further up the same street where we were going.

We stopped right in front of the lottery agency. It closed at 9:00, and we had just missed it. "Finding it closed means for me to forget it. It is not supposed to be here," I told my friend. We then went to the liquor store to get Paula's alcohol. While I waited for the clerk to put some camphor into the liquor (this way it would be unfit for drinking, so we wouldn't have to pay liquor tax to take the alcohol into the United States), my friend went to a back room where he found some lottery tickets.

Success at last

"What numbers are you looking for?" my friend called from the adjoining room. I told him, and he called back, "3-4-3 is here."

I said, "You are kidding me, are you not?"

My friend then answered, "Come and see."

Sure enough, there were five segments of an active series numbered 3-4-3. A complete series contained 20 segments. Someone had already purchased the other 15 segments. My friend asked what I was going to do. "Buy these, of course!" I told him. So I bought them. I had never ever thought of buying lottery tickets, but I bought five segments and would find out in two days if the number 3-4-3 would win anything.

I found out that the ticket with the numbers 3-7-3 had been sold in Mexico City. It could not have been found anywhere else because 3-7-3 was assigned to be sold in Mexico City only. If I had purchased that ticket, I would have cleared, after paying the Mexican income tax, about $1,000.

On the other hand, 3-4-3 was assigned to be sold by the liquor store in Nuevo Laredo, and nobody else in the whole Republic of Mexico could have had it. The 3-4-3 had a prize also, and after paying the Mexican income tax and exchanging the Mexican pesos into U.S. dollars, I cleared a little more than $10,000 with just my five segments on the ticket. I came home dazed, with $10,000 in my pocket—and in 1949, that was a lot of money!

Why did this happen?

In trying to figure out who had put that number in my head and why, I went back over my experience step by step, and found many coincidences. For example, my wife wanted a bottle of alcohol from Mexico. I could have told her I'd get it the next time I made a service call. Or I could have asked her to send someone else. Instead I went that night. Paula did not know about my experience, much less know that she was sending me to the one place in the entire Republic of Mexico where the ticket was sold.

And what timing! If my friend had come only 10 minutes later, I would have left already. If my friend had not gone with me, I would not have thought of buying a lottery ticket, let alone walked into the other room and seen the tickets. And even if I had thought about the lottery, I would not have continued to look for the tickets after finding the lottery agency closed.

After backtracking and after going over every detail of the experience, I found myself faced with many coincidences. I felt that those coincidences were trying to tell me something, or that somebody was trying to tell me something through those coincidences. I then felt that I must seek and find out what it was that I was supposed to do, or not do.

I started going back prior to having the experience, hour by hour, step by step, seeking a clue. The only thing I saw that could have had a connection and could have brought on the series of coincidences was the decision I made to stop studying psychology.

With that realization, I pulled the psychology book out from under the couch, dusted it off, and continued studying.

This chain of coincidences—not just one coincidence, but five coincidences on the same subject—is what I consider divine intervention.

Verification and confirmation

Scientists always look for verification. Having all of those coincidences happen the way they did provided me with the verification that it was divine guidance.

I believe that a spontaneous event with detrimental end results is an accident, and that a spontaneous event with beneficial end results is a coincidence that could be divine guidance.

A series of beneficial coincidences is surely divine intervention.

Many people in Laredo would have thought about the lottery immediately, just as my friend did. If I had thought about it, I would have checked the lottery agency immediately, which means that I wouldn't have found the ticket.

High intelligence guided me, through the series of coincidences, to the right place, so that I would find the lottery ticket, and would understand that it was not just luck or coincidence, but divine guidance.

My many coincidences with the lottery-ticket experience was a means of getting back on track.

From then on I started experimenting, trying to put together a method that would help to enhance what I used to call "the guessing faculty." What I called "the guessing faculty" turned out to be the psi—or intuitive—factor.

ADDING TO THE FORMULA FOR SUCCESS

Thus another element was added to the formula for success: information from higher intelligence; it is not always just your own ability to detect information on other people's neurons.

My father developed a course that he taught for the next 30 years, following the path he had taken in his research: He started by teaching people how to use more of their minds for personal improvement, and then introduced them to their own natural psychic abilities. People were amazed and thrilled with their newfound abilities. They quickly went to work using the self-improvement techniques every day. And on special occasions they used their ESP to help them with special situations.

My father's quest: If ESP is not a special ability, but a natural human function that we all have, then it should not be set aside for special occasions, but should be used every day just like any other natural ability that we have.

So, once again, his approach mirrored what he had done earlier. He shifted his focus from helping me and my brothers and sisters with the self-improvement skills and began to concentrate on two areas: (1) begin to use ESP as a natural part of our everyday lives; and (2) seek more guidance and help from higher intelligence.

"Just remember," he told us in the summer of 1997, "that the reason we were given ESP is so that we can use it to find out what we were sent here to do, and how to do it successfully."

In other words, we can manifest the coincidences in our lives that will reveal to us our purpose in life, and will guide us to success in that mission.

THE NEXT STEP

After more than 30 years of experience with the Silva Method, a new system was revealed to him.

At the age of 82, he was not interested in developing a new course, but several members of his family began to pressure him to modernize the original course in ways that they thought might be more acceptable to the general public. He didn't want to start doing new research into what would work best for a more modern course, so he decided that he would just take his original research in a new direction. Once he had opened up to that idea, he was inspired to develop a new technique that is far better than anything from the past: the MentalVideo.

For the next two years, his work evolved into something much more than just a course. He called it a *system*.

The Silva UltraMind ESP System is the course my father would have liked to have taught in 1966, but people were not ready for a course that promised to train them to be psychics with a higher purpose. They were primarily interested in helping themselves.

The original Silva Method moved many people from a "me-centered" approach to a "we-centered" attitude. One of the first beneficial statements was this: "My increasing mental faculties are for serving humanity better."

Other statements were primarily me-centered. "Positive thoughts bring me benefits and advantages I desire" and, "every day in every way I am getting better, better, and better" are good examples.

The statements in the new UltraMind System are all we-centered:

o "Do unto others only what you would have others do unto you."

- o "The solution must help to make this planet a better place to live."
- o "The solution must be the best for everybody concerned."
- o "The solution must help at least two or more persons."

Thanks to my father and the system he developed, humanity has experienced a shift in consciousness. People now understand that they are not just physical beings, but are physical and spiritual. People now understand that the tools of their spiritual nature are visualization, imagination, and psychic ability. They understand that we are all connected to one another, and we must all work together.

Today, people are eager to develop their psychic abilities so that they can connect spiritually with other people and project mentally to correct problems.

In the remainder of this chapter and in the next three chapters, my father will provide step-by-step guidance for you to learn to enter a deeper level of mind, so that you can develop and use your psychic abilities.

In Section II, there is information on how to use the alpha level to expand your capabilities, and to communicate directly with higher intelligence.

The rest of the book provides everyday examples of people using their Everyday ESP in every area of life: health, relationships, and business. One of the best ways to learn is to learn by example, so we will provide you with plenty of examples of what people did and how they did it, so that you can get the same kind of, and even better, results in your life.

Now let's get started by explaining the alpha brain-wave level, and giving you your first alpha experience.

WHAT IS ALPHA?

Your "bio-computer" brain operates on a small amount of electricity, just as a personal computer does. It can process and store information, retrieve that information, and then use that information to make decisions and solve problems.

Unlike other computers, the electricity that the brain generates and functions with does not remain at a fixed frequency. Sometimes this electric current vibrates rapidly—20 times or more per second. Other times it vibrates very slowly—one time or less per second. Scientists call these vibrations cycles (or hertz), and have divided the brain frequency spectrum into four different segments, based on the number of cycles per second (cps).

- o Beta is above 14 cps, typically 20 cps when your body and mind are active and you focus your eyes.

- o Alpha, from 7 to 14 cps, is associated with light sleep and dreaming.

- o Theta, from 4 to 7 cps, is associated with deeper sleep, and with the use of hypnosis for such things as painless surgery.

- o Delta, less than 4 cps, is associated with deepest sleep. In the next chapter, we'll talk more about the delta level and how you can use it for two-way communication with high intelligence.

DEVELOPING THE ALPHA LEVEL

During his research in the 1950s, my father reasoned that the best range to use for mental activity would be the range that has the least impedance and the most energy. Not only did most scientists disagree, but they doubted that it was even possible for people to learn to remain at the lower alpha brain frequencies once they activated their minds.

My father proved them all wrong.

The alpha frequency is the strongest (as far as currency) and the most rhythmic of the four. That's why it was the first to be discovered by scientists with their primitive sensing equipment; it was named "alpha" for the first letter in the Greek alphabet.

Until now, delta has been a big mystery to researchers. People lose awareness when the brain frequency lowers to delta. Now, for the first time, we have a technique to allow us to use the delta level purposefully.

HOW PEOPLE USE THEIR MINDS

It seemed logical to my father that the alpha level would be the ideal level to do your thinking, if you could learn to actually activate your mind while at alpha.

- You could think more clearly, because it provides more energy.

- You could maintain your concentration better.

- You could access more information, more easily, because it is in the absolute center of the brain's normal operating range.

But here's the catch: Research revealed that most people do their thinking at the beta frequency!

Most people, when their brain frequency slows to alpha, enter the "subconscious" area and then fall asleep. Most people are using the weakest, least stable frequency to do their thinking: the beta level. But the super successful people stay awake at the alpha level and do their thinking there.

YOUR FIRST ALPHA EXPERIENCE

Will you invest a few minutes a day to learn to enter the alpha level with conscious awareness? If you will do this, and then will learn to apply the techniques of the Silva Method, then you will succeed. We'll provide step-by-step guidance, so you will know exactly what to do.

It is easier to do it than to explain it, so let's get right to your first mental training exercise, also known as a conditioning cycle. For that, read the instructions in my father's words:

In the two-day Silva training programs, attendees learn how to function consciously at alpha in just a few hours, because they have the help of a trained lecturer who guides them step by step and answers all of their questions. Since you are going to be learning by reading this book, it will take longer. It will take you approximately 40 days if you do it completely on your own with the countdown deepening exercises. It will take you about 10 hours of practice if you use the audio recording on the CD that came with this book. If you have already attended a live Silva seminar, then you already know how to enter and use the alpha level.

I will give you a simple way to relax, and you will do better and better at this as you practice.

I will also give you a beneficial statement to help you.

This is how you train your mind. You relax, lower your brain frequency to the alpha level, and practice using imagination and visualization.

Because you cannot read this book and relax simultaneously, it is necessary that you read the instructions first, so that you can put the book down, close your eyes, and follow them.

Here they are:

1. Sit comfortably in a chair and close your eyes. Any position that is comfortable is a good position.

2. Take a deep breath, and as you exhale, relax your body.

3. Count backward slowly from 50 to 1.

4. Daydream about some peaceful place you know.

5. Say to yourself mentally, "Every day, in every way, I am getting better, better, and better."

6. Remind yourself mentally that when you open your eyes at the count of five, you will feel wide awake, better than before. When you reach the count of three, repeat this, and when you open your eyes, repeat it ("I am wide awake, feeling better than before").

You already know steps one and two. You do them daily when you get home in the evening. Add a countdown, a peaceful scene, and a beneficial statement to help you become better and better, and you are ready for a final count-out.

Read the instructions once more. Then put the book down and do it.

THE MAGIC OF THINKING AT ALPHA

Thanks to my father, you have just experienced "programming."

Your ability to program improves with practice. With practice, you relax more quickly and reach deeper, healthier levels of mind; you visualize more realistically; and your levels of expectation and belief heighten, yielding bigger and better results.

Programming in this manner at the alpha level produces far better results than programming at the beta level. You can repeat positive statements a thousands times at the outer level and not have as much effect as you can with just one repetition of a positive, beneficial statement at the alpha level. That is why some people are able to visualize their goals and then reach them, while most people get very few results.

Our research found that only about one person in 10 naturally thinks at the alpha brain wave level and acts at the beta level.

Now you will be one of the one-in-10. Remember, the only way to get superior results is to learn how to function at the alpha level with conscious awareness, the way the 10-percenters do.

USING THE ALPHA LEVEL CONSCIOUSLY

As stated previously, you learn to enter the alpha level and function there with just one day of training when you attend the Silva UltraMind ESP Systems live training programs. You can use the audio recordings to learn to enter the alpha level within a few days with either a Silva home-study program or the CD included with this book.

If you have already learned to enter the alpha level by one of those methods, you can skip the following instructions for practicing countdown-deepening exercises for the next 40 days.

If not, then follow these instructions from Jose Silva:

When you enter sleep, you enter alpha. But you quickly go right through alpha to the deeper levels of theta and delta.

Throughout the night, your brain moves back and forth through alpha, theta, and delta, like the ebb and flow of the tide. These cycles last about 90 minutes.

In the morning, as you exit sleep, you come out through alpha, back into the faster beta frequencies that are associated with the outer-conscious levels.

Some authors advise that as you go to sleep at night, you think about your goals. That way, you get a little bit of alpha time for programming. The only trouble is, you have a tendency to fall asleep.

For now, I just want you to practice a simple exercise that will help you learn to enter and stay at the alpha level. Then, in 40 days, you will be ready to begin your programming.

In the meantime, I will give you some additional tasks that you can perform at the beta level that will help you prepare yourself so that you will be able to program more effectively at the alpha level when you are ready at the completion of the 40 days.

Your first assignment

Following the Silva Centering Exercise (also known as the Long Relaxation Exercise) on the enclosed CD, enter the alpha level, and skip the information that follows.

If you do not want to use the recording of the Silva Centering Exercise, and you have not attended a Silva seminar or used one of our home-study courses to learn to enter the alpha level, then you will need to follow the instructions here to learn to enter the alpha level on your own.

Here is your alpha exercise:

Practice this exercise in the morning when you first wake up. Since your brain is starting to shift from alpha to beta when you first wake up, you will not have a tendency to fall asleep when you enter alpha.

Here are the steps to take:

1. When you awake tomorrow morning, go to the bathroom if you have to, then go back to bed. Set your alarm clock to ring in 15 minutes, just in case you do fall asleep again.

2. Close your eyes and turn them slightly upward toward your eyebrows (about 20 degrees). Research shows that this produces more alpha brainwave activity.

3. Count backward slowly from 100 to one. Do this silently; that is, do it mentally to yourself. Wait about one second between numbers.

4. When you reach the count of one, hold a mental picture of yourself as a success. An easy way to do this is to recall the most recent time when you were 100 percent successful. Recall the setting, where you were and what the scene looked like; recall what you did; and recall what you felt like.

5. Repeat mentally, "Every day in every way I am getting better, better, and better."

6. Then say to yourself, "I am going to count from one to five; when I reach the count of five, I will open my eyes, feeling fine and in perfect health, feeling better than before."

7. Begin to count. When you reach three, repeat, "When I reach the count of five, I will open my eyes, feeling fine and in perfect health, feeling better than before."

8. Continue your count to four and five. At the count of five, open your eyes and tell yourself mentally, "I am wide awake, feeling fine and in perfect health, feeling better than before. And this is so."

THESE EIGHT STEPS ARE REALLY ONLY THREE

Go over each of these eight steps so that you understand the purpose while at the same time become more familiar with the sequence.

1. The mind cannot relax deeply if the body is not relaxed. It is better to go to the bathroom and permit your body to enjoy full comfort. Also, when you first awake, you may not be fully awake. Going to the bathroom ensures your being fully awake. But, in case you are still not awake enough to stay awake, set your alarm clock to ring in 15 minutes so you do not risk being late on your daily schedule. Sit in a comfortable position.

2. Research has shown that when a person turns the eyes up about 20 degrees, it triggers more alpha rhythm in the brain and also causes more right-brain activity. Later, when we do our mental picturing, it will be with your eyes turned upward at this angle. Meanwhile, it is a simple way to encourage alpha brainwave activity. You might want to think of the way you look up at the screen in a movie theater, a comfortable upward angle.

3. Counting backward is relaxing. Counting forward is activating. 1-2-3 is like "get ready, get set, go!" 3-2-1 is pacifying. You are going nowhere except deeper within yourself.

4. Imagining yourself the way you want to be—while relaxed—creates the picture. Failures who relax and imagine themselves making mistakes and losing, frequently create a mental picture that brings about failure. You will do the opposite. Your mental picture is one of success, and it will create what you desire: success.

5. Words repeated mentally—while relaxed—create the concepts they stand for. Pictures and words program the mind to make it so.

6–8. These last three steps are simply counting to five to end your session. Counting upward activates you, but it's still good to give yourself "orders" to become activated at the count of five. Do this before you begin to count; do it again along the way; and again as you open your eyes.

Once you wake up tomorrow morning and prepare yourself for this exercise, it all works down to three steps:

1. Count backward from 100 to 1.

2. Imagine yourself successful.

3. Count yourself out 1 to 5, reminding yourself that you are wide awake, feeling fine, and in perfect health.

40 days that can change your life—for the better

You know what to do tomorrow morning, but what about after that? Here is your training program:

○ Count backward from 100 to 1 for 10 mornings.

○ Count backward from 50 to 1 for 10 mornings.

○ Count backward from 25 to 1 for 10 mornings.

○ Count backward from 10 to 1 for 10 mornings.

After these 40 mornings of countdown relaxation practice, count backward only from 5 to 1 and begin to use your alpha level.

People have a tendency to be impatient, to want to move faster. Please resist this temptation and follow the instructions as written.

You must develop and acquire the ability to function consciously at alpha before the mental techniques will work properly for you. You must master the fundamentals first. We've been researching this field since 1944, longer than anyone else, and the techniques we have developed have helped millions of people worldwide to enjoy greater success and happiness, so please follow these simple instructions.

Chapter 2
The Correct Depth

People tend to follow those who demonstrate that they are guided by a higher power to make the correct decisions and achieve great success in their endeavors. Religious leaders gain followers. Businesspeople build great business empires.

Many successful people listen to the "little voice inside" and reach lofty goals.

People have long recognized the value of having this ability, even if they have to fake it. There have been instances of people who do not actually have this ability, but who pretend to have it, such as the evangelists who use sleight of hand to make it appear as if they can actually heal people on the spot in order to gain followers and the monetary contributions they bring.

The problem is, while some people have had this ability, they have not been able to pass on a method that the ordinary person could use to gain this same kind of ability, to learn to do it, too.

They don't know what it is about themselves that is different, that gives them the ability to do this. They know how they function, and assume that everybody else functions the same way. Why would they think differently? They have only their own experience on which to draw.

The followers have been so busy following the leaders that, even if they somehow pick up some clues and develop this ability themselves, they do not learn enough to be able to pass on this knowledge to anyone else. And the naturals who have this ability are usually not even able to pass it on to their own children.

Napoleon Hill's laws of success

At the beginning of the 20th century, a newspaper reporter named Napoleon Hill met one of these geniuses who had been guided to achieve success: Andrew Carnegie, a steel magnate, was the wealthiest person in the world.

Carnegie advised Hill that there was something different about the super-successful people. He knew a lot of super-successful people personally, as well as a lot of ordinary people, and he knew that they were different.

So he made a proposal to Hill: If Napoleon Hill was willing to make a study of these people and determine what the differences were, Carnegie would secure appointments for Hill with these super-successful individuals.

During the next 20 years, as Hill interviewed these people, he identified several characteristics that the super-successful people had in common. By far the most important, Hill discovered, was their ability to sense information with their minds, an ability the average person did not possess.

"If you can find a way to stimulate your mind to go beyond this average stopping point," Hill said in his *Reading Course on the Law of Success* (published in 1928) "fame and fortune will be yours." Hill understood that psychic ability was the foundation of everything, especially if you could also connect with a higher power for guidance.

Although Hill apparently developed these abilities himself, he never found a way to teach them to others. He could teach people all of the other laws, but he was never able to unlock the secret of how to teach people to develop and use their intuition on demand.

The key to unlock the secret of success

From 1944 to 1966, my father conducted research to learn why some people were so much more successful than the average, such as he had been, so that he could teach this to his own children.

Early in his research, my father looked to religion to see what it said on the subject. He was born into a Catholic family in a Catholic community, so his first investigation was into Catholicism. He wanted to be sure that the techniques he was experimenting with did not violate any of the teachings of his religion.

He found that they did not conflict. The teachings of Jesus both supported what he was doing and gave him ideas for additional experiments. "It has always seemed to me that Jesus was guiding me to the discoveries that I made," my father said.

While this offered some assurance, it was not enough for my father. He realized that if he had been born into some other religion, he would have looked to that religion for clues to success. So he took time to study all religions. "I studied the origin of each religion," he said, "when it was founded and who founded it. I wanted to know what their beliefs were, their philosophies. I wanted to know what their goals were."

What he discovered was pretty amazing. "I saw that all religions were trying to accomplish the same thing," he said. "It reminds me of what somebody once said, that all paths lead to the same God."

MANY PATHS TO THE SAME DESTINATION

In fact, religious leaders throughout history have said much the same thing. Here are some examples:

- In the fifth century B.C., Lao Tse said, "The broad-minded see the truth in different religions; the narrow-minded see only their differences."

- More than 300 years before Christ lived, Aristotle said, "God has many names though he is only one being."

- The New Testament of the Bible seems to agree: "There is neither Jew nor Greek, there is neither bond nor free, there is neither male nor female: for ye are all one in Christ Jesus" (Galatians 3:28).

- The Koran offers an explanation as to why people see things differently, even if all religions are trying to achieve the same thing: "Every child is born into the religion of nature; its parents make it a Jew, a Christian, or a Magian."

So it was a Jewish rabbi named Jesus, who, through the writings in the Bible, provided some of the most important clues in my father's search for the "secret of success."

Now it is all available to you. No matter what your religion, no matter what you believe, this will work for you. The Silva Method does not violate any religion's belief, nor does it violate any scientific principle.

The Silva Method holds the unique position of being consistent both with religious philosophy and scientific method. My father, a simple man from a small town deep in southern Texas, without any formal education, achieved what no one else has: he has brought science and religion together.

FINDING THE CORRECT DIMENSION

You have already started the mental exercises necessary to find the correct dimension for applying the self-management techniques that you will find in Section II of this book, and for developing your psychic ability.

If you have graduated from one of the Silva seminars or completed a Silva home-study program, then you have already learned to enter your level, and you do not need to use these countdown exercises for this purpose.

However, it is still valuable to practice the countdown-deepening exercises in order to ensure that you maintain your level. Learn to activate your mind while maintaining this level in order to use the self-management techniques and your psychic ability.

EXPLORING A WHOLE NEW DIMENSION

This great dimension, accessed by super-successful businesspeople and religious leaders alike, must be explored by examining brain waves and levels at which different people function. Scientists have divided brain activity into four groups: alpha, beta, theta, and delta.

The alpha frequencies are the strongest, most energetic, most stable, and most synchronous frequencies. This makes the alpha level the ideal level to do our thinking, the level where there is the least impedance to the flow of electrical activity. This would also indicate that the center of the alpha range, at 10 cycles per second, is the fundamental frequency.

Beta is the weakest, least stable of the four frequency ranges. It is the ideal level when we are physically active. We can use our energy for physical activity rather than brain activity.

When we are physically active, we typically function at 20 cycles beta, which would be the first harmonic of the alpha frequency. The 5 cycles per second frequency in the theta range would be the first sub-harmonic.

Unfortunately, 90 percent of people do both their thinking and their acting at 20 cycles beta. The 10 percent who do their thinking at 10 cycles alpha and their acting at 20 cycles beta are the ones who are the most successful. They are healthier, they seem to have good luck, and they achieve more in life.

The theta level, from 4 to 7 cycles per second, is a much more passive level. You cannot use it to analyze information and solve problems. At alpha and beta you can function deductively—you can analyze and reason. At theta, you can only function deductively. If you activate your mind, your brain will speed up to the first frequency that it has learned to use with conscious awareness. For 90 percent of people, that is 20 cycles beta, the least effective level to do your thinking. For the 10 percent who naturally maintained the ability to use the 10 cycles alpha frequency as they matured, and for people who have learned the Silva Method, the brain will stop at 10 cycles per second.

The theta frequency is associated with biological intelligence—the "control panel" for the body, so to speak. Hypnotists can give suggestions at that level for things such as painless dentistry and painless childbirth. Once you learn to function at 10 cycles alpha with conscious awareness, you can learn to give yourself those kinds of suggestions. For that to be effective, you need to practice enough so that you learn to enter the theta level on your own with conscious awareness; then when you program from the alpha level, your programming will be effective at theta when necessary.

There is one more frequency range that scientists identified long ago, and that is the delta area, from .5 to 5 cycles per second. But scientists could learn very little about delta, because very few people could go there with conscious awareness.

Delta is associated with deep sleep. For most of us, the only way to get to delta is by going to sleep. If you are hit in the head and knocked unconscious or if you are anesthetized with chemical anesthetics, you will go to theta. So scientists have not had a way to conduct research at the delta level to analyze it and determine what it is there for.

Some people have had a sense of what it is for. Yogis, for instance, typically want to go to the lowest frequencies possible in their attempt to unite with God. The word *yoga* actually means "yoke" (the apparatus you would use to join two oxen together to pull a cart) or "union." They say that their goal is to be joined with God. They have an instinctive understanding that this somehow involves the lowest delta, frequencies.

My father came across some interesting bits of information concerning the delta frequency. He learned that delta is the first human-type brainwave frequency detected in the fetus, while still in the mother's womb. When the child is born, the brain runs up and down the scale through all of the frequencies, as if to check out the hardware to make sure it will function correctly. Anyone who has raised children knows that infants sleep much of the time. Research shows that their overall predominant brain frequency is in the delta range.

As children grow older, their overall predominant brain frequency increases. It typically matches the child's age: A 5-year-old child's overall predominant brain frequency is 5 cycles per second. At 10 years old, when children are very imaginative and creative, the overall predominant brain frequency is 10 cycles per second. A mature adult's overall predominant brain frequency is usually 20 cycles per second.

My father also learned that as a person nears death, and dies, the last active brain frequencies are the delta frequencies. It is like completing a cycle. It seems as if the delta frequencies are used when we first come into this life, and are also used as we leave our earthly life and return from whence we came.

My father dubbed this the Delta Doorway. Delta, he said, is the doorway we use to come into the world, and the doorway we use to leave and go back to wherever we came from.

When the very first delta frequencies are detected in the developing fetus, this is an indication that human intelligence (what some people call the "soul" or "consciousness") enters the body. Human intelligence enters the body and uses the brain to operate the body as a puppeteer would operate a hand puppet.

The body is created in the physical dimension. Human intelligence comes from a spiritual dimension; one we sometimes call that the "other side." My father used to compare this working together to astronauts being sent to the moon. When they get to the moon, they have to put on their heavy space suits in order to survive and carry out their work in that environment, much as human intelligence has to have a human body in order to survive and carry out its work in the physical dimension.

Astronauts also need the ability to communicate back to Mission Control in order to get instructions and to carry out their mission properly.

The scientists in Houston (Mission Control) are the ones who want the information about the moon, and who want certain types of material brought back. In order for the astronauts to do their job properly, they need to communicate with Mission Control for guidance. If they run into a problem, then they need to get instructions from the engineers about how to correct the problem.

Likewise, we need to communicate with the "other side" to obtain guidance as to how to best carry out our mission here on planet earth.

When my father put it all together, he realized that our communication with the other side has to go through the Delta Doorway.

And when do we have access to the Delta Doorway? During the deepest sleep at night.

Through the years, we have had several nighttime techniques. Some we use before going to sleep. Other times, we program ourselves to wake up during the night at the ideal time to program. Sometimes those techniques produce "inspired" answers and solutions.

Once my father put it all together, he knew what to do to "improve the communication with higher intelligence," as he put it. He always believed that he was guided in his research every step of the way, "and that's putting it lightly," he said. For years he wanted to understand how the process worked, and how to improve it so that we could communicate regularly and reliably, and get answers and guidance that we could use to help us carry out our assignment here on planet earth.

A little more than a year before he made his own journey back through the Delta Doorway to the other side, he developed the MentalVideo Technique. I wish that he were here to see and enjoy the results that people are getting with it. Perhaps he is observing by way of the reports we send back to the other side with the use of the MentalVideo.

In Chapter 6 he will teach you the MentalVideo Technique so that you can start using it immediately. Then, throughout the rest of the book, you will read many examples and case studies about how people have been using the MentalVideo, and the results they are getting, so that you will know how to use it in your life to carry out your mission successfully.

But first, you must learn to function at alpha so that you can correct problems that could prevent you from using the MentalVideo Technique effectively.

OVERCOMING OBSTACLES TO DELTA

What could prevent you from using this technique effectively?

Sleeping pills, for one thing. When you use sleeping pills to go to sleep, then the drugs try to take control of your central nervous system. The drugs prevent you from going through the normal 90-minute cycles associated with sleep and dreams.

And to the extent that the drugs prevent you from entering the delta level, you are precluded from using the MentalVideo Technique effectively.

Drugs always have side effects. If you are taking medication for migraines, for instance, or for other kinds of pain, those drugs will have side effects. They often interfere with the normal functioning of your central nervous system.

Habits such as smoking or drinking also have undesirable side effects.

At deep levels of mind, you can gain control over these and other problems.

The most powerful exercise for doing that is the Silva Centering Exercise (also known as the Long Relaxation Exercise). My father will explain it to you starting on page 41. His brother, my Uncle Juan Silva, felt that the best way for people to learn to help themselves was to learn the Long Relaxation Exercise and to use it on their own. Those people who were willing to do that, he felt, would get the greatest benefit. "Nobody else knows as well as you what it takes for you to relax," he explained. "Nobody else knows as well as you where you hurt."

Even if you learn how to enter the alpha level by practicing the Silva Centering Exercise in class or from a recording, we still recommend that you learn it well enough so you can do it on your own, and continue to practice it at least once a week to ensure you maintain your level.

We do not use any physical means to relax the body; we use the mind. "You can have a relaxed body with an active mind," he explained, "but you cannot have an active body with a relaxed mind." That's why you learn to use your mind to relax your body, and then you also relax your mind. That is how to find the alpha level.

I will now turn the rest of the chapter over to my father to teach you how to do that.

PHYSICAL AND MENTAL RELAXATION LEAD TO ALPHA

Physical relaxation

Once you feel that you are able to maintain your concentration during your daily countdowns, you're ready to learn to relax with the Long Relaxation Exercise.

To do this, I want you to use your mind to relax your body. And then I want you to relax your mind. When you do this, your brain will relax into the alpha level.

Here is how to proceed with the first part, using your mind to relax your body:

Find a comfortable position. Let your body do what it wants to do in order to be comfortable. However, I do not want you to fall asleep; if you fall asleep during this exercise, then make yourself a little less comfortable and do it again.

When you have found a comfortable position, then close your eyes.

Why do I ask you to close your eyes? Several reasons:

Whenever you attempt to focus your eyesight, your brain automatically goes to 20 cps beta frequency. You can use all of your other senses while you are at alpha, but not your eyesight. So I do not want you to focus your eyes or try to "see" anything while you are at alpha.

Now I want you to mentally repeat and visualize the number 3 several times. To make this easy to do, get a piece of paper before you begin, write the number 3 on it; then just recall what it looks like. We will associate the number 3 with physical relaxation.

The next thing that I want you to do is to imagine your body relaxing from the top of your head to the soles of your feet. Here is how to proceed:

First, concentrate your attention on your scalp, the skin that covers your head.

You will sense a fine vibration, a feeling of warmth caused by circulation. Use your imagination for this. Do not just wait for it to happen by itself; imagine what it would feel like. Imagine that you can actually feel it.

Now release and relax all tensions and ligament pressures from this part of your head completely, and place it in a deep state of relaxation that will continue to grow deeper and deeper as we continue.

What will your scalp feel like if it is completely relaxed? Will it feel like a warm dishcloth lying over your skull? Will the roots of your hair be gently washed in the warm flow of blood in your scalp?

Use your imagination to sense your scalp relaxing. Then do the same thing with the rest of your body.

Your forehead, the skin that covers your forehead—concentrate your attention on your forehead; you will detect a fine vibration, a tingling sensation, a feeling of warmth caused by circulation. Then release and relax all tensions and ligament pressures from this part of your head completely, and place it in a deep state of relaxation that will grow deeper as we continue.

Your eyelids, and the tissue surrounding your eyes. We have great control of the eyelids, so allow them to relax. It is important to realize that you do not "force" yourself to relax; you "allow" yourself to relax.

Your face, the skin covering your cheeks.

Your throat, the skin covering your throat area.

Within the throat area.

Your shoulders. To help you concentrate on your shoulders, concentrate on and "feel" the clothing in contact with your shoulders.

Your chest. Again, feel your clothing in contact with your chest.

Within the chest area—relax all organs, relax all glands, relax all tissues including the cells themselves, and cause them to function in a rhythmic, healthy manner. How do you do this? You use your mind—your imagination—the same as you do for the skeletal muscles.

The abdominal area.

Within the abdominal area.

Your thighs.

At this time, I want you to do something extra. Sense the vibration at the bones within the thighs; by now these vibrations should be easily detectable. Go ahead and sense them.

Your knees.

Your calves.

The toes of your feet.

The soles of your feet.

The heels of your feet.

Now you have gone from head to feet, using your mind to direct your motor nerves to relax your muscles, and even your internal organs.

Now I want you to relax your sensory nervous system as well. I want you to be so relaxed that you are not even aware of your body, not aware of sensory information coming through your sensory nerves.

Here is how:

Cause your feet to feel as though they do not belong to your body.

Cause your feet, ankles, calves, and knees to feel as though they do not belong to your body.

Cause your feet, ankles, calves, knees, thighs, waist, shoulders, arms, and hands to feel as though they do not belong to your body.

This is your physical relaxation level three.

Now I would like for you to mentally repeat and visualize the number 3 several times, to associate this feeling of relaxation with the number 3. In the future, whenever you desire to relax physically, as relaxed as you are now, just mentally repeat and visualize the number 3 several times, and you will relax physically as you are now, and even more so.

Mental relaxation

Next, mentally repeat and visualize the number 2 several times. The number 2 is for mental relaxation, where noises will not distract you. In fact, noises will help you to relax mentally more and more. You may be aware of noises and distractions, but your desire will cause you to disregard them and relax mentally more and more.

Mental relaxation is very simple: To relax mentally, simply recall tranquil and passive scenes.

Any scene that makes you tranquil and passive will help you to relax mentally.

You may find that you are very relaxed after strenuous physical activity, such as a fast game of tennis or some such similar activity. But this is not what we want here.

I want you to recall something where you are passive, relaxed, and not moving around very much. Just enjoying yourself.

A day at the beach may be a tranquil and passive scene for you.

A day out fishing may be a tranquil and passive scene for you.

A tranquil and passive scene for you might be a walk through the woods on a beautiful summer day, when the breeze is just right, where there are tall shade trees, beautiful flowers, a very blue sky, an occasional white cloud, birds singing in the distance, even squirrels playing on the tree limbs. Hear birds singing in the distance.

Remember to associate this level with the number 2.

Enter the alpha level

After you are completely relaxed both physically and mentally, repeat and visualize the number 1 several times, and take it for granted that you are now at level one, the alpha level, a level that you can use for a purpose, for any purpose you desire.

If you have graduated from one of the Silva seminars or have used the recordings in the Silva home-study program, then you can do this immediately.

If you are brand new to the Silva System and are learning by practicing the countdown exercises every morning, then your first goal is to learn to maintain your concentration during the countdowns. If this is difficult for you, practice until you get the hang of it.

Then you can begin to use the Silva Centering Exercise, also known as the Long Relaxation Exercise.

I recommend that you practice the Silva Centering Exercise once a week for the next three months.

Of course, you can practice more than that if you wish. Many Silva graduates continue to practice the Long Relaxation Exercise for many years, to insure that they maintain a deep, healthy level of mind.

They do this because it helps the body to maintain vibrant good health, and it is necessary in order to use the 3-Scene Technique in Chapter 5. It is also the level that is required for psychic functioning.

Now continue to practice, either with the recording of the Silva Centering Exercise, or practice the 100 to 1 countdowns each morning for the next 10 days.

Thank you.

Chapter 3
The Correct Attitude

In order to obtain guidance and help from high intelligence, it is important that you have the correct motive for doing so.

What is the correct motive?

Is high intelligence going to help you in order for you to have a wonderful life, to get everything you want, to enjoy yourself?

Will high intelligence help you to gain at somebody else's loss? Will high intelligence help you to take prizes and deprive your opponents of winning them?

We do not think so, and the evidence supports us.

We believe that the correct reason for seeking help is so that you can use the help and guidance that you receive to do the job you were sent here to do.

And what is that job? To correct problems, and, by so doing, to perfect the creation and convert planet earth into a paradise.

COMMON SENSE GUIDES US

If we want a higher power to help us, then we have an obligation to do what the higher power wants us to do.

Several years ago, a beer company advertisement theorized that "you only go around once, so grab all the gusto you can." But that attitude doesn't make much sense.

There is an obvious parallel in our lives: If you work for someone and that person pays you to do a job, then you have to do the job, or else he will fire you and stop paying you.

Well, that's a good theory, but is there any evidence to support it?

And, more importantly, is there a way that we can actually determine what our jobs are? Is there a way to find out what task higher intelligence has assigned to each of us?

Fortunately, the answer to all three questions is: Yes! Yes! Yes!

My father learned very early in his life that the more you give, the more you get back. His research and study of successful people confirmed that over and over.

JOSE SILVA LEARNS HOW TO GET MORE MONEY

After my grandfather died and my grandmother remarried and moved away, my father, then 6 years old, found himself the oldest male in the family, and he felt an obligation to earn enough money to support his sister and younger brother. He asked his uncle for guidance, and he helped my father set up a shoeshine business.

He learned that men would pay him to shine their shoes. The more shoes he shined, the more money he made. The better job he did, the more repeat business he got.

Then one day he asked his uncle, who was helping him, why so many men were looking at those big sheets of paper. His uncle explained that they were reading the newspaper to learn what was going on in town. So my father found out where to get newspapers and offered them for sale to his customers.

And he made more money by doing that.

When he overheard some men talking about how difficult it was to find an honest, reliable person to clean their offices at night, he offered to do it. He was so enthusiastic about it that they decided to give him a chance.

They tested him by leaving a watch and some money out. He put the items away, and the next day he went in and showed the men where he had put them. They knew they could trust him, and they saw he would do a good job, and so he made more money.

It's logical: The more people you serve, the more service you provide, the more problems you solve, the more rewards you will receive.

THE ATTITUDE THAT MADE THE SILVA METHOD POSSIBLE

There's no better proof of this logic than the Silva Method itself.

The more people my father helped with what he was learning in his research, the more *he* learned.

It is as though the other side was giving him more information as they confirmed that he was using it not for selfish purposes, but to correct problems.

He never accepted any money for what he did; he was happy to do it.

And he was rewarded. The other side found a way to get $10,000 to him once in the early 1950s, to let him know that he should continue his research, by way of a lottery ticket. (He told that story in Chapter 1.)

Unfortunately, some people think that the Silva Method is just about getting things for yourself. There have been instructors who have tried to market the course that way. But, in the course, you learn that my father had something else in mind.

UNDERLYING PRINCIPLE OF THE SILVA UltraMind ESP System

The first Beneficial Statement used in the Silva Centering Exercise is: "My increasing mental faculties are for serving humanity better."

You are advised that your mental faculties are increasing, and at the same time you are advised of what your obligations are.

How could a person not want to help someone who is hurting? How can anyone just walk away when he or she sees somebody in need?

If you were not taught this when you were young, or if you have outgrown those natural instincts to help and to do constructive and creative things, then start working on getting to deep levels of mind. Get back to a level—brain-wise—before you were contaminated, before fear and insecurity distorted your natural instincts and judgment.

That's what the Silva Centering Exercise does for us: It takes us back on the scale of brain evolution to an earlier age—when we were young and the brain functioned predominately at alpha—and reprograms us with these statements. It is almost as if you are going back and changing your past. If you were not taught properly, now you can go back and do it right!

WHAT MAKES SUCCESSFUL PEOPLE DIFFERENT?

My father conducted more research on success than anyone else in history. He was the first person ever to use the electroencephalograph (EEG) to actually study the brains of people and determine what separates the super-successful from the ordinary.

What he found is that super-successful people do their thinking—get information and make decisions—at the alpha-brain level. He used to ask people questions while he had them connected to the EEG, and noticed that most people would remain in beta by observing their brain waves when they answered questions. But a few—about 10 percent—would first dip into alpha, and then they would come back to beta to answer the questions.

After this happened a number of times, he realized that the people whose brains dipped into alpha—apparently to obtain and analyze information there—tended to be more successful than those whose brains remained at beta. Evidently there was more information available at alpha than at beta.

A NEW ATTITUDE

My father's research went way beyond this discovery. He observed that the people who experienced the most success in *all* areas of life—not just financial, but health, relationships, happiness, sense of satisfaction, and so on—had a different attitude than the average person.

He continued to research and observe people, and this research, along with his own experience and the experiences of people who followed his guidance, convinced him that there is a certain attitude that is necessary for success.

His advice was always to program to provide service, and keep in mind what your needs are, plus a little bit more. He said that we should be helping to convert the planet into a paradise.

When we develop these wonderful innate mental tools, we should be using them to correct problems—without being concerned about whether we are compensated for this work or not.

If my father had not worked for 22 years without ever accepting a penny for his efforts, we would not have the Silva Method today.

Based on his research and his experience for more than half a century, he felt that if we are only trying to help ourselves, or if this is our main focus, then we are on our own, we are not going to get any help from high intelligence. But if we are working to correct the problems of humanity—because that is the right thing to do, because this is what we were sent here to do—then we will qualify for help from high intelligence.

DO IT BECAUSE IT IS RIGHT, NOT FOR WHAT YOU WILL GET

We know people who will do anything to help anyone as long as there is something in it for them. But that's not sufficient. Anything that you program for should benefit at least two people. That's the minimum; the more the better.

If you are just working for yourself, and doing things for yourself only, then you are not likely to get help from higher intelligence. You are on your own. The techniques will still work for you, but it is much easier when you have help from other graduates and from high intelligence.

Worry about obtaining money—or "the love of money" as a preacher would say—causes much suffering. John D. Rockefeller Sr. was probably the wealthiest man in the world, but he worried so much about gaining more money that it destroyed his health. His doctor told him that his money was going to kill him, and that's when the senior Rockefeller became a philanthropist.

John D. Rockefeller Jr. later observed, "Giving is the secret of a healthy life. Not necessarily money, but whatever a man has of encouragement and sympathy and understanding." In an address at Fisk University he said, "I believe that every right implies a responsibility; every opportunity, an obligation; every possession, a duty."

The Koran agrees that it is *our duty* to help those who need our assistance, with more than our prayers: "Woe be unto those who pray, and who are negligent at their prayer: who play the hypocrites, and deny necessaries to the needy."

You do not have to be wealthy to help others. "Even the beggar who lives on alms should himself bestow alms," the Babylonian Talmud suggests.

You can see an example of how all of us can help others in the story of Marge Wolcott a little later in this chapter. She could not sit up by herself, and she had to have a brace on her neck to hold her head up, and still she spent much of the day helping others.

You have probably heard the saying that if you give a person a fish, he will satisfy his hunger for a day; but if you *teach* him to fish, he can feed himself from now on.

The Talmud agrees: "The noblest charity is to prevent a man from accepting charity; and the best alms are to show and to enable a man to dispense with alms."

Not an easy challenge, but one that my father accepted. The Silva UltraMind ESP System gives you the tools, the guidance, and the direction that you need to take care of yourself, and to help others also.

Many graduates start by working on themselves in order to remove the impediments that could be distracting them from their life's mission, such as correcting health problems and getting rid of bad habits. This is quite natural. A lot of graduates have great success doing this.

Then they turn their attention to things such as earning more money, getting a raise, improving their position, and attracting the ideal mate. All of these things involve other people. If you want to improve your position within humanity, then you need to work just as hard to correct the problems of humanity as you would work to correct your own personal problems. The truth is, the problems of humanity *are* your problems. When you lift up humanity, you are also lifting up yourself, because you are a part of humanity.

A CORRECT ATTITUDE LEADS TO SUCCESS

What my father realized, as he studied both unsuccessful and successful people, as he studied the ancient writings and at the same time worked with thousands of people, was that *a correct sense of values* is an important factor in success.

In fact, this was very important to my father in his very important work as a holistic faith healer. Here is what he wrote about the necessity for a correct sense of values in his autobiography (*The Autobiography of Jose Silva*, Institute of Pyschorientology Inc., 1983):

I would ask the patient some questions, such as, "Do you really want to be healed?" and I would add, "because my time is very valuable and I do not intend to waste it."

Of course the answer was, "Yes, I want to be healed." Some even felt insulted by my asking such a question.

My next question was, "Why do you want to be healed?"

If the answer was, "To be a better wife (or husband, or son, or daughter) and help by being a perfect human being who will help solve the problems of my neighborhood, my city, state, or nation," there was no more to say. I would go to work and help the patient.

But if the answer centered on how the patient needed to live it up, enjoy life, not helping anything or anybody, then I would try to straighten out the patient's way of thinking before starting the healing.

We realize that not everybody is ready to accept all of these ideas. That's fine. Feel free to study them, and take as long as you need. As we say in the Silva Standard Conditioning Cycle, "You may accept or reject anything I say, any time, at any level of mind."

Once you learn to analyze information while at the alpha level, these ideas will make more sense to you.

How a Chicken Ruined Two Families

My father believed that it is very important that we understand what's really important in life. Years ago, two of his neighbors in Laredo got into a silly argument about chickens that had tragic consequences.

One neighbor had a small garden in the backyard. The other neighbor had some chickens. One day, one of the chickens jumped the fence and damaged some of the plants in the neighbor's garden. The two women got into an argument about the damage. Should there have been a better fence? Was the homeowner responsible for the actions of the chicken?

When their husbands got home at dinnertime, both wives were upset and wanted their respective husbands to take some kind of action. The two men got into an argument, which led to one man shooting and killing the other.

What a tragedy! One husband dead, the other in prison, two women raising their children alone, children deprived of their fathers, the loss of two wage-earners—the tragic consequences go on.

We *must* learn to put things into perspective and focus on what's really important in our lives.

WHAT IS IMPORTANT?

It is important that we fulfill our missions in life. And we submit for your consideration that your mission seems to be to correct problems and help make our world a better place to live.

Why do we feel that way? Two reasons:

1. Our observations of successful people.

2. People who follow this path experience success.

We know people who put themselves at the center of their own worlds. We know people who work 20 hours a day, who stay focused on their goal and let nothing dissuade them, people willing to win at any cost. We've seen them make a lot of money, but the money still didn't really make them happy.

We're not saying that money keeps you from being happy. We know people who are constantly doing for others, sacrificing, and giving, who never have enough for themselves, and they aren't very happy, either. They feel as if they have been shortchanged. And, in a sense, they have.

We must always have a balance. There is a relationship between what we give and what we get.

My father's formula for prosperity and abundance is simple: Program to correct problems and make the world a better place to live, and keep in mind what your needs are, plus a little bit more.

DO YOU "PREY" OR DO YOU "PRAY"?

Let's take a practical example to show the difference between one who preys on others for personal gain only, compared to one who is doing what is best for everybody concerned: Suppose you want to sell or buy a house. You contact a few real estate agents. If the first agent who comes to see you is desperate for money and will do anything to make that commission, it is not in your best interest.

The second agent is determined to make the best deal for all concerned, even if it takes a little longer, and even if it means a slightly lower commission.

Which one do you want to deal with? Which one has your best interest at heart? Which one are you going to refer to your friends? Who is going to end up with the most customers? The selfish one or the selfless one? You know the answer.

Sometimes, from a beta (left-brain) perspective, it may seem as though we should be trying to get everything we can for ourselves. But from an alpha (right-brain, or spiritual) perspective, we see otherwise.

According to my father, we prey *on* each other at the beta level, but we pray *for* each other at alpha.

Keep in mind that you must have a balance—you give, and you also receive. If you do not permit the people to whom you give to compensate you, then you are cheating them of the wonderful opportunity to gain all of the benefits of giving. Be unselfish—keep a balance in your life between giving and receiving.

You can determine the value of your work based on the compensation that you receive.

COMPENSATION COMES IN MANY WAYS

There is not always a direct relationship between giving and receiving: When you do $5 worth of work for somebody, you may not receive $5 compensation from that person. But overall, you will be compensated.

Read my father's story about a time when he healed a man in Mexico:

I crossed the Rio Grande River three times a day, every day, for a month, to perform the "laying on of hands" to correct a health problem that the man had.

At the end of the 30 days, the illness was gone.

One of my friends, who had doubts about helping somebody without requiring them to pay for the help, told me, "I'll bet he didn't even offer to reimburse you for the bridge tolls, did he? How much did it cost you to go over and treat him almost 100 times?"

I figured out that it cost me approximately $500, but added that it did not matter, that my needs were being taken care of.

That night, I did not have any appointments, so my wife, Paula, asked me to go to the church recreation hall with her to the bingo game.

Although I was not interested in playing bingo, I knew that I should spend some time with my wife, so I accompanied her there. Naturally, I participated in the game.

Guess who won the big jackpot that night?

I did!

Guess how much the jackpot was?

It was $500.

The next day, I called my friend and told him about winning the $500. "Maybe that is the way high intelligence sees to it that we are compensated," I told him.

"Oh, you and your strange ideas!" my friend said. He just didn't understand.

HOW TO WIN FRIENDS

Would you want to do business with somebody who was only interested in how much he can get for himself? Would you want to marry a person who only wanted to get all they could from you?

If you are dedicated to helping humanity, without expecting to be directly compensated for it, then everyone will want to be associated with you, do business with you, and be your friend.

You don't need to spend any money to find people who need help and to program for them.

When you help other people, especially people who are hurting badly, then you will have many successes. You will be improving your skills a great deal. This is like anything else; the more you practice, the better you get.

But my father always cautioned that we should not practice just for what we will get out of it; we should correct problems because that's what we're sent here to do.

If you give to get something, you're not giving, you're trading. Your motives are second in importance only to your actions.

DOING WHAT'S BEST FOR ALL CONCERNED

Here is a real-world example of how programming in a calm, relaxed way while taking other people's feelings and needs into consideration can bring spectacular results. Here is an experience that an Indonesian resident named Abel had:

> I want to share a recent wonderful experience I had.
>
> I was on a vacation with my wife and sons recently. We were supposed to fly back on the 15:30 flight on Saturday, but on Friday afternoon the

airline called to inform that the flight was canceled due to some technical problems. We were then given seats on the next flight available at 20:30 hours on Saturday. I asked for an afternoon flight on the Sunday but was told that there were no more seats available. I reluctantly agreed to the 20:30 flight on Saturday.

On Friday evening, I went out with my friends and their parents. When their parents learned of my rescheduled flight, they strongly advised me to avoid the 20:30 flight for safety reasons, and they even asked me to reprimand the airline for the schedule change so that I would be guaranteed seats on the afternoon flight. So I called the airline and courteously asked for the afternoon flight on Sunday, but the best that they could give me was the 06:30 flight on Sunday and placed me on a waiting list for the afternoon flight just in case someone cancelled. That was somehow better, and I agreed.

Deep in my heart, I knew my chances of getting seats on the afternoon flight were slim, as it coincided with the end of the Moslem holidays and traffic would be heavier than normal. Naturally, everyone would choose to take the afternoon flight rather than the early morning or late evening flights, yet my only chances were on other passengers' cancellation, and worse still I needed four passengers to cancel so that I could fly together with my wife and sons, and surely there were other people on the waiting list before me.

So that Friday night before I went to bed I ran through my dilemma, and having done that, I then went to alpha. I pictured my family and I going to the airport in the afternoon and taking the afternoon flight home. I pictured the event vividly, seeing my sons waving at my friends who took us to the airport. After a few minutes, I counted out and then went to sleep.

The next day, just before lunch, I received a call from the airline informing me that they were able to put my family and me on the afternoon flight on Sunday.

I was so happy then that I told my wife about my going into alpha the night before. I kept it from her at first, fearing that things would not turn out as I pictured it to be. That was certainly an awesome experience. I am keeping it in mind to strengthen myself for subsequent centering to solve problems and receive help from the Other Side.

I want to emphasize that I was all polite and courteous to the airline personnel I spoke to, expecting their full cooperation and assistance.

Never once did I become angry or scold them for having rescheduled my flights. Secondly, all along during the visualization process, I kept a thought that I wouldn't be getting those seats at the expense of others' misfortune, hence leading them to cancel their flights.

That reminds me of how my father used to quote Napoleon Hill about sharing your programming with other people: Hill said that telling other people about your goals is like punching holes in a boiler and letting all the steam out. When people don't believe you, then it lets all the energy out of your programming, so only tell those who understand what you are doing and will help you and reinforce your own programming.

MAKING SENSE AT THE SUBJECTIVE DIMENSION

At deep levels of the mind, people seem to understand this without any problem. So if this seems like too strange a concept to you, then practice deepening your level until you get back to the level before you were contaminated, to a time when things were more pure, clean, and positive.

In meditating on these ideas, my father found a Bible verse that the subjective dimension seemed to him to sum up the whole thing: "Seek ye first the kingdom of heaven, and function within God's righteousness, and all else will be added unto you" (Matthew 6:33).

In our model, the Kingdom of Heaven represents alpha. God's righteousness represents doing what God wants—correcting problems and improving conditions on planet earth. All else represents everything you need, plus a little bit more.

If you need a million dollars, it's easy to get. Just give $10 million worth of service to humanity, and if you *need* a million dollars, you'll get it.

PRAYING FOR OTHERS HELPS OVERCOME INCURABLE ILLNESS

People who understand the principle that we are all connected here on planet earth, and that whatever affects one human being affects all of humanity, are the people who achieve miraculous success.

Marge Wolcott attended the Silva Method Basic Lecture Series in Laredo taught by Ed Bernd Jr. in February 1982. She was a very religious person, who was accustomed to praying for other people's health. Here is her story, in her own words, as she told it to Ed:

I had multiple sclerosis (MS) for 15 years. When I came to the Silva Mind Control lectures, I was wearing a body brace and a neck brace. I had to bring in a special chair to sit in.

When I came to Silva Mind Control, I had strong faith, but it was doubled after I finished the Basic Lecture Series.

Two months after graduating, I took the neck brace off. Two months after that, the body brace broke, across the back and shoulder area. My daughter, who had taken the Mind Control course with me, suggested I quit wearing it. She knew I had been tempted to take it off.

I tried it, and have not worn it since. In fact, later, a doctor from Dallas who had a crippling illness and had to close his practice, came to visit me. I didn't know it then, but he knew a lot about MS, and said later he could not detect any signs that I'd ever had it!

He took Mind Control, recovered, and reopened his practice, I heard.

After I recovered from the MS, I saw my doctor again. His only comment was that he'd heard of this kind of thing happening, but this was the first time he had ever seen it. He had felt there was no hope of my recovering. I had worn the brace about seven or eight years.

Here's what I did, using the Silva Mind Control Method:

I programmed three times a day. Many people were calling me, asking me to help them, so I would go to level three times a day to program for them.

Since I was programming for them, I'd also program for myself after I had finished programming for them.

I knew the doctors felt there was no hope for me, so I had little hope myself. I had desire, of course, and I would not have bothered programming if I had not had some expectancy that it could help. But I was not concerned about it. If I got better, that would be great. If not, I could accept that.

The Bible says that whatever you do for others comes back to you tenfold. Apparently, when I programmed for the other people, I was helping myself, too. The thoughts of healing seemed to have influenced my own brain to make corrections in my own body.

It has been 12 years since I graduated from Silva Mind Control, and I have had no trouble since then with the MS.

One of the challenges I had at that time was severe pain in my face muscles. When I heard about the Headache Control Technique, it felt like someone placed a hand on my shoulder. The pain in my face stopped and has not been back since.

Also, ever since I graduated, I have used the "better and better" phrase. I use it all of the time and feel sure that it has been a big help to me in my programming and my success with the Silva Method.

Notice that Marge spoke very little about programming herself. Many people want to know how she visualized, how often, and other similar things. What she told us—what she considered important—was that she was using what little energy she had, and the short time she felt she had left on this earth to program for as many other people as she could, and also kept in mind what her needs were.

FORMULA FOR SUCCESS

My father gave us a formula that covers this. It is the formula for prosperity and abundance, for self-confidence and self-esteem, for happiness and contentment. It is in a paragraph that is found at the very end of the Silva Centering Exercise. It reads like this:

You will continue to strive to take part in constructive and creative activities to make this a better world to live in, so that when we move on we shall have left behind a better world for those who follow. You will consider the whole of humanity, depending on their ages, as fathers or mothers, brothers or sisters, sons or daughters. You are a superior human being; you have greater understanding, compassion, and patience with others.

Let's take a detailed look at this paragraph.

AN INTENTION TO CORRECT PROBLEMS

You will continue to strive...

Some people question the use of the word *strive*. They think it is like the word *try*, and that *try* is a negative word.

Well, it can be negative or positive, depending on how you use it.

What's really important is the mental picture that you are creating. Suppose you are very busy, and you have other priorities ahead of this particular thing that you would like to do. You can say, "Okay, I'll do it!" But that can put a lot of pressure on you and make you feel bad if you don't manage to get it done. Perhaps that works for some people.

Or you can say, "I doubt if I'll have time to get to it." What kind of mental picture does that create?

Maybe a better way is to leave the door open by saying, "I've got a lot of things to do, but I'll certainly try to get this done, too."

What mental picture does that create? The idea of doing it stays in the back of your mind, and perhaps your mind, subconsciously, guides your actions so that you are now able to accomplish the task.

HOW TO KNOW THE DIFFERENCE BETWEEN RIGHT AND WRONG

...to take part in constructive and creative activities to make this a better world to live in...

A lot of good people today seem to be confused about the concepts of right and wrong. My father tried to make this plain and simple by talking about doing constructive and creative work.

Figure out what your purpose in life is. To help figure it out, ask yourself this: When you were a young child, what kind of things did you do that made you feel good about yourself? Enter your level and think about it. What can you do that needs to be done?

President John F. Kennedy said that happiness comes from doing worthwhile work that you are good at and that you enjoy doing.

Sometime when you have a few minutes, do what my father used to do: Get out a dictionary and look up some words, particularly the words he uses, words such as constructive, creative, good, honest, pure, clean, and positive. Meditate on them.

THE HIGHEST—GODLY—MOTIVE

Back to my father's instructions:

...take part in constructive and creative activities to make this a better world to live in so that when we move on, we shall have left behind a better world for those who follow.

That seems like a strange instruction, doesn't it?

When Ed asked him if that was a statement of unselfishness, my father answered simply, "If it had not been for that attitude, we would not have the Silva Method today."

He never accepted payment of any kind for his efforts to help people during the entire 22 years of his research. He would not even allow people to reimburse him for expenses, such as gasoline and bridge tolls. Interestingly enough, Napoleon Hill conducted research of successful people for more than 20 years without receiving any money, even for expenses, before he put together his Law of Success Course. It has been said that you have to give before you receive.

A SPECIFIC ASSIGNMENT ON OUR JOURNEY

...when we move on...

Now there's an interesting phrase. We don't just put in a few decades of work, and then everything comes to an end. Our responsibilities continue as we move on to whatever comes next for us.

Do not let the fear of failure stop you from trying.

Please don't think that we are saints. We're ordinary folks who make our best efforts, and sometimes we come up short. Like the old saying goes, it's not how many times you fall down, it's how many times you get back up.

There was a young gymnast in the 1996 Summer Olympics who made two terrible mistakes. Her team was going for the gold, and she had asked the coach to let her anchor the team. She said she was strong enough to go last, so she could see what was needed to win, and then go get it. Her coach agreed.

The athlete who competed before her, her training partner, fell on both of her vault attempts.

After watching that, Kerri Strug made her first attempt and fell exactly the same way as her training partner had done. That's a perfect example of the way that "mind guides brain, and brain guides body." In this case, Kerri Strug saw an imperfect performance and didn't get it out of her consciousness, so she duplicated it.

Kerri had one attempt left, and only needed an average score to beat the second-place Russians. But she had made the one mistake that an athlete simply cannot afford to make: she had injured herself, spraining her ankle on her first vault. She couldn't even walk on the ankle, much less run fast enough to gain enough speed to complete her vault.

But the coach told her to shake it off. "I couldn't shake it off," she said later. But she made the attempt anyway, and somehow managed to keep her form through all the pain, and "nailed" the landing—winning the gold medal for the U.S. women's Olympic team for the first time in decades.

Kerri Strug was an instant hero, the most famous athlete to emerge from the 1996 Olympic Games.

But think about this: If she had simply done her first vault correctly and gotten the necessary points to win the gold, we wouldn't even remember her name today. She'd just be one member of the team. She didn't score any perfect 10s, she didn't do anything to distinguish herself—until she made that terrible mistake and injured herself, when she was the last hope for her team to win the gold.

If she hadn't made the mistake, she wouldn't have been the hero.

Heroes are not people who always do great things. Heroes are people who persevere, who hang in there, who are not afraid to try—to strive—and to make mistakes—and to fail—and then to come back to try, try again.

A BLUEPRINT FOR CORRECT SERVICE

The next idea touches on the popular idea that we are all brothers and sisters here on planet earth.

You will consider the whole of humanity, depending on their ages, as fathers or mothers, brothers or sisters, sons or daughters...

For many years, there have been people who promoted the concept of "the brotherhood of man." By the 1960s, amidst the struggles for equal rights for all people, including women, people began to recognize that we are all "brothers and sisters." My father was ahead even back then. He was already emphasizing that our relationships go beyond treating everyone as a peer.

Do you accord people who are old enough to be your parents the same respect and patience that you would give to your own parents? Do you turn away from an old person who needs help because you are busy, or do you do what you would do if it were your own father or mother?

Do you respond in the same way to your peers as you would your own brothers and sisters? Brothers and sisters may fight with each other, but they still love each other. Can you do that with other people as well?

What about young people? In a business situation, would you take advantage of someone who is young and inexperienced? Or would you help that person, nurture and teach him or her, the same as you would your own son or daughter?

WE ARE CARETAKERS

You are a superior human being. You have greater understanding, compassion, and patience with others.

As humans, we are the highest life form on this planet. According to my father, we are like gods on this planet; we can do the same things on this planet that God can do throughout the Universe.

If we do a good job while we are on this planet, we will be promoted and will be given larger responsibilities and opportunities when we move on.

Think of those words: understanding, compassion, and patience. Look them up in the dictionary. Meditate on them at your level. And program yourself to let them guide you.

YOUR NEXT ASSIGNMENT

In the next chapter, we will give you some suggestions and guidelines about how to practice in order to deepen your level and make sure that you maintain it so that you can use it any time you need it to help you make decisions, correct problems, and achieve your goals.

Before we get to that, here are two assignments for you:

1. Meditate on what has been written in this chapter. Think about your attitude, your motivation, and your purpose in life. We live our lives on the choices we make. Be sure to make the best choices possible.

2. Continue to practice with the Silva Centering Exercise or with your countdowns in order to establish a good deep alpha level from which to function.

Chapter 4
Practicing

Now that you have been practicing with the recording of the Silva Centering Exercise or with the countdown exercises (on pages 41–44) to learn to enter the alpha level, or have completed a Silva seminar or home-study course, you are ready to use the alpha level to correct problems and achieve your goals.

In addition to learning to enter the alpha level, it is important to maintain that level. That means practice. Here are the recommended ways in which you should practice.

HOW TO ESTABLISH A GOOD FOUNDATION

Use the 3-to-1 method to enter your level.

Remain at your level for at least five minutes. Ten minutes is better, and 15 minutes is excellent.

What do you do during that time? You can practice deepening exercises, such as countdowns from 25 to 1, 50 to 1, or 100 to 1. You can practice relaxing. You can project yourself mentally to your ideal place of relaxation, a place where you have been before and have been physically passive and relaxed. You want to bring back into your mind a very vivid memory of a time when you were passive and relaxed. This will trigger a "conditioned response"—that is, your brain will try to recreate in your body the conditions that existed at that time. This means that your body will relax.

You can also review the projects you are working on, imagine succeeding at them, and recall how you will feel when you do.

The best time to practice is in the morning when you wake up. Your brain is just coming out of the alpha stage, so it will be easy to go back there. Because it is morning and time to get up, you will not be as likely to fall asleep as you will be at bedtime.

The second best time is at bedtime. Your brain is ready to go to the alpha level when you go to sleep, so it will be easy to get there.

The third best time is just after lunch. It is natural to feel relaxed and a little drowsy after eating. When you relax after a meal, it is easier for your body to digest food. It is also easy to enter alpha.

Be sure that you stay awake during the time you spend at alpha. If you fall asleep, you do not get the benefits of alpha-functioning. This may take some practice. Do whatever is necessary to learn to remain awake while at alpha. Make yourself less comfortable. Raise your hand; holding your arm up will help to keep you awake. If it starts to fall, you will become alert again.

At the same time, you do not want to become too active mentally. That could bring you out of your level. So, from time to time, check yourself out and make sure that you are still physically and mentally relaxed. To be sure, use a deepening exercise: Count down from 10 to 1, or relax your eyelids and let the feeling of relaxation flow slowly down throughout your body all the way down to your toes, or visualize tranquil and passive scenes.

Once you feel relaxed and comfortable, continue with your programming.

As you continue to practice and notice your results, you will become very proficient at doing this, and confident in your ability to know when you are at your level.

My uncle Juan Silva used to tell us that the best time to practice is when you don't need to.

Why is that?

Because that is when it is the easiest to do. When you are not under stress, it is easy to relax and enter the alpha level.

Then later, when you encounter a stressful situation and need to enter the alpha level to calm yourself, and to correct the problem, it will be automatic.

Hector Chacon, head basketball coach for 30 years at my old high school, Martin High, taught a group of average players how to use the 3-Scenes Technique, which you will learn in the next chapter, to visualize themselves playing at a superior level. He has a wonderful way of explaining it:

When there are two seconds left in the game, and we are 3 points behind, and I have a player at the free throw line ready to shoot two free throws, I don't want him thinking about making those free throws. I want that to be automatic. I want him to be thinking about how we are going to get the ball back after he makes the two free throws so that we can shoot another basket and win the game before the two seconds expire.

When you are under stress, you don't want to spend your time thinking about how to go to the alpha level. You want it to be automatic, so that you can get to work correcting the problem.

Coach Chacon proved that he knows what he is talking about. The very first year he taught his players how to go to level with the Silva Centering Exercise and visualize themselves winning, they won the Bi-District Championship. Before the season started, the "experts" picked his team to finish *no better* than fifth out of seven teams in the district.

ADVICE FROM A NATURAL ALPHA-THINKER

While working on this book, we came across a book by a natural alpha-thinker who had a special gift when it came to explaining what he did. Anyone who can function at the alpha level can benefit from his writings. The author is Robert Collier, and many of his books are still available from his family.

There is a paragraph in Collier's book *Riches Within Your Reach: The Law of the Higher Potential,* published in 1947, just three years before his death, that answers a question that many Silva graduates have asked over the years: "Why is it when I have a really strong desire for something, and I really *need* it, and it will benefit many people, and I program *really hard* for it, I still don't get results? I get great results on little things that are not so important; why not this?"

Collier's guidance expresses one of the main principles that my father incorporated into the UltraMind ESP System: We do all that we can to fulfill the plan that higher intelligence has for us.

Here is the way Robert Collier said it:

Look at the first chapter of the Scriptures. When God wanted light, did He strive and struggle, trying to make light? No, He said—"*Let* there be light."

When you want something very much, instead of trying to make it come your way, suppose you try asking for it and then *letting* it come. Suppose you just relax, and *let* God work through you instead of trying to *make* Him do something for you. Suppose you say to yourself "I will do whatever is given me to do. I will follow every lead to the best of my ability, but for the rest, it is all up to the God in me. God in me knows what my right work is, where it is, and just what I should do to get it. I put myself and my affairs lovingly in His hands, secure that whatever is for my highest good, He will bring to me."

My father said we were sent here for a purpose, with a job to do. If we fulfill that purpose, then we will be happy, fulfilled, and prosperous. Now you know how to program to fulfill your mission successfully.

Do it the easy way

We have a Silva UltraMind ESP System instructor in Dallas named Temple Nash who has an interesting way of expressing things. Here is how Temple explains this same concept:

That has to be one of the most difficult things to teach anyone, to *let* things happen. Everybody wants to "make things happen," what a crock. Those who are amazed at the results I get can't begin to grasp the concept. I let criminals catch themselves, it is so much easier that way. Like I told a kid in Corsicana, "It is much easier to load live hogs on a trailer than it is to load dead ones." Let things happen, don't force them. Too much work!

Now let me turn the floor over to my coauthor, Ed Bernd Jr., to tell you the extraordinary story about how he was guided, or perhaps shoved, to this information.

Guidance in action

One of the things that has mystified us for years is why programming sometimes works so well, and other times we just can't seem to get results no matter how hard we try.

There have been situations where we programmed for something that seemed nearly impossible, and then pretty much forgot about it, and next thing we know we got results.

Other times we programmed for simple things that we thought would be easy to accomplish, and no matter how many people joined in the programming and no matter how often or how hard we tried, we didn't get anywhere.

I also recall times that we would be working hard with Jose Silva on a project, overcoming obstacles as they cropped up, then overcoming more obstacles, and suddenly he would tell us to back off and stop fighting it. "If it is meant to be," he would say, "then it will happen." I would ask him about persistence and desire and all those things you read about in the "success" books, and he would just repeat, "If it is meant to be...."

We tried to imitate him, but we never quite understood what he was doing. Silva graduates had the same question about why they sometimes failed to get results even though they put a lot of time and effort into their programming.

Then one hot Saturday in August of 1999 here in Laredo, six months after Mr. Silva had died, I picked up my 70-year-old friend Daniel, and we went to the local flea market. We were getting ready for our annual international convention and also instructor training, it was 110 degrees (F) outside, and I was tired and didn't want to stay very long.

We always checked out all of the sellers. At the very back of the grounds, there were no stalls, just dozens of cardboard boxes on the ground, filled with a wide variety of items. As I walked among the boxes looking down at them, a book caught my eye, an old hard cover book that was published in 1950. On the cover were the words "Riches within Your Reach," with horizontal lines above and below the words. A very simple design, silver imprint on a dark blue background.

When I opened the book I saw it was by Robert Collier, who was both an extremely intuitive and spiritual individual, and a direct marketing (mail order) genius who often pushed the limits in his aggressive marketing. At the time, I thought to myself that there must have been something about the design of the book that caught my eye.

I bought the book for about 10 cents, and we headed back across the large grounds toward the entrance to the flea market. Just inside the entrance there was a produce stand run by a very nice and hard-working old man. Daniel wanted to get some fruit, but the old man was not at the stand. He often walked through the grounds to take produce to the vendors because they needed to stay near their stalls in order to sell their merchandise.

So we sat down to wait. I wasn't very happy about that. I was hot and tired and had many things to do to prepare for the convention, instructor training, and other activities that were starting in just a few days. But Daniel wanted to wait. So I sat down in the old man's chair and we waited. No sign of the old man. So finally I decided to read a little bit of the book. I hoped that would distract me from my annoyance, because I didn't want to hurt Daniel's feelings.

The beginning of the book was great, typical Robert Collier material that gets you excited and makes you think. Still no sign of the old man, so I kept reading, even though I really wanted to leave.

Then I got to page 33. That extraordinary paragraph quoted on page 67–68 was the last paragraph on the page. There was nothing else, not even a single line after the end of that paragraph.

I was overwhelmed by the information conveyed by that one paragraph. It seemed to answer so many of the questions that we'd had for more than 20 years. I read the paragraph over again, and then again, and yet again. And I silently thanked Daniel for insisting on waiting for the produce man to return so he could buy some food.

Eventually, the produce man returned, we bought some food from him, and left. I dropped Daniel off and went home and read that paragraph again. That night in my MentalVideo I thanked higher intelligence for guiding me to that book, and for keeping the old man away from his produce stand long enough for me to get to page 33, because I probably would not have read it to this day if not for that.

I don't know what is in the rest of the book, because I have not gone past page 33. Perhaps there is another gem waiting for me. If so, I hope someone lets me know. Somebody said that God works in mysterious ways, and I was pushed around, shoved around, and annoyed in order to get me to read enough of the book to find the information that has been so valuable to us.

Robert Collier died in 1950 while Jose Silva was just beginning his research into ESP. We can only imagine what might have happened if Jose Silva, with his unparrelled insights, and Robert Collier, with his amazing gift for explaining spiritual principles in such a clear way, had gotten together.

PREPARE YOURSELF FOR SUCCESS

In the next chapter we will show you a simple technique that you can use to correct problems and remove impediments to your success.

Meanwhile, continue practicing, either with the recording of the Silva Centering Exercise or with the daily countdown deepening exercises.

Section II: Expand Your Capabilities

Chapter 5
Program With Images

Before the development of alphabets and sophisticated languages of various kinds, people communicated with pictures. Those ancient cave-drawings can be understood by modern people just as easily as they could by primitive people long ago. No matter what language you speak, you can still recognize their pictures of animals, trees, rivers and streams, and even people. Those pictures often tell stories about what happened to the people of that era.

Good communicators use words to create mental images in their audience's minds. An average communicator, for example, might say, "It's time for young people to exercise some leadership." President John F. Kennedy, a great communicator, said, "The torch has been passed to a new generation of Americans."

Mental pictures—in the form of visualization and imagination—can be one of the most powerful tools you can use in your mental programming. Pictures are the universal language. Everybody, no matter where they live or what their backgrounds are, will "get the picture." They understand. Writers spend hours trying to describe what something looks like. A picture makes it easy.

We need to send regular reports to higher intelligence to let our helpers in the spiritual dimension know what is happening in the physical dimension, and what we are doing about it. Mental pictures have proven to be the best form of mental communication.

UNDERSTANDING VISUALIZATION
AND IMAGINATION

When you hear the phrase "the torch has been passed," what does that look like to you? What kind of torch would you imagine? If you were looking at the event, what would you see? Where is the person who is passing the torch—to your left, your right, facing you, with his or her back to you? Where is the person receiving the torch? Is it a man or a woman passing the torch? What about the person receiving the torch? An adult? A child? How is he or she dressed? Describe how you would you have them dressed if you were directing this scene in a film.

That's all that we need when we talk about mental pictures. If you can think about what something looks like, and can describe it, you are doing it correctly.

In order to help us understand this better, let's define some terms the way that we use then in the Silva programs:

- o **See.** You see with your eyes.

- o **Visualize.** When you recall what something looks like
  that you have seen before, you are visualizing. It is the
  memory of what something looks like. It is not the same
  as seeing; it is not nearly as vivid. Most people say that
  dreams are more vivid than visualization. You can
  visualize with your eyes open or closed, at beta or at
  alpha. Just relax and recall what something looks like.

- o **Imagine.** Imagination is a creative process. When you
  imagine, you think about what something looks like
  that you have never seen or imagined before.

If you have seen someone pass a torch to another person and you recall what that looked like, that's visualization. If you do not recall something you have seen before, but make up your own scene, that's imagination. Later, when you recall that scene you created with your imagination, you are using visualization, because you are using memory to recall something you experienced previously.

Words can often help you to create better mental pictures. You might want to describe a scene to yourself to help you recall it or imagine it. For instance, think of a relative or friend that you know very well and think of what his or her face looks like. It might help you to recall the color of the person's hair, skin, and eyes, and what his or her forehead, nose, cheeks, and facial characteristics are.

If you are visualizing a project you are working on, it might help you to imagine that you are discussing the project, and how to go about doing it in order to help you create a detailed mental picture of it.

Just remember that your words are there to *support* your mental images, not to substitute for them.

ESTABLISHING A COMMUNICATIONS SYSTEM

My father developed the concept of the Mental Screen to use as a communications tool. If you want to examine an existing situation to determine what the problem is, project an image of it onto your Mental Screen so that you can make a good study of it. Then when you are ready to correct the problem, you project the solution image onto your Mental Screen.

To locate your Mental Screen, begin with your eyes closed, turned slightly upward from the horizontal plane of sight, at an angle of approximately 20 degrees. The area that you perceive with your mind is your mental screen.

Without using your eyelids as screens, sense your Mental Screen to be out, away from your body.

Your eyes should be turned upward to a comfortable position, but not so far as to be uncomfortable. Turning your eyes upward in this manner increases the amount of alpha brain-wave activity.

Using the Mental Screen is the easiest way to detect information, and it is also the easiest way to transmit information. In the physical world, you receive information with your ears, and you transmit information with your voice. In the spiritual dimension, you receive information with visualization, and you transmit information with imagination.

The Mental Screen can be as large as you want it to be. It can surround you if you like, so that you can observe things from all angles. You are in control and can make it what you want it to be.

CORRECTING PROBLEMS WITH VISUALIZATION AND IMAGINATION

You can use the 3-Scenes Technique to correct problems and to achieve your goals.

When you desire to use the 3-Scenes Technique, go to your center (the alpha level) with the 3-to-1 method. Create and project onto your mental screen, directly in front of you, using visualization, an image of the existing situation.

Recall details of what the situation looks like in this first scene. Make a good study of the existing situation so you are completely aware of all aspects of it. When my father said to make a good study of the problem, he meant that we should observe the details.

If you have programmed for this project previously, then take into account any changes that have taken place since your most recent programming session.

After making a good study of the existing situation, shift your awareness to your left, approximately 15 degrees. In a second scene, to the left of the first scene, use imagination to mentally picture yourself taking action and doing something to implement your decisions, and to follow the guidance you have received, and imagine the desired changes beginning to take place.

Now in the third scene, another 15 degrees farther to your left, use your imagination to create and project an image of the situation the way you desire for it to end up. Imagine many people benefiting. The more people who benefit, the better.

Anytime in the future when you think of this project, visualize (recall) the image that you created of the desired end result in the third scene.

When you shift your attention toward your left to create the solution image, this takes into account the passage of time from a subjective point of view. Research has revealed that from a subjective point of view, the past is to your right, the present is in front of you, and the future is to your left.

SOME PROGRAMMING TIPS

When you program, look for objective feedback to let you know what effect your programming is having. We recommend that you program in such a way that you would expect something to happen within the next few days.

If you notice an improvement in the project within two or three days, then you know to keep on programming the way you have been doing. If the situation gets worse in the next two or three days, then go to your level and analyze what happened. You might realize that you should alter your programming.

When you are not getting positive results, try anything that you can think of at your level to see if you can change things and start making progress. Sometimes you need to program more; sometimes you need to program less.

Perhaps the problem can be summed up with the sentiments in the quote from Robert Collier mentioned in Chapter 4: Sometimes we are trying so hard to *make* something happen the way we think it should happen that we block ourselves. Instead, try to *let* it happen. Release it, so that higher intelligence can do whatever is best for all concerned.

The more desire you have, the better. How many reasons do you have for wanting to correct this problem? Perhaps there are five benefits that you can think of. Enter your level and think about it again; you might come up with five more benefits. Then you will have twice as much motivation.

"The bigger your project is," my father told us, "the more help you will get from higher intelligence. What I mean by bigger is how many people will benefit. If you are just programming something for yourself only, then you are on your own; you're not going to get any help. But if your programming will benefit many people, then you will get help. The more people who will benefit, the more help you will get."

The more you practice, the better. Begin by entering your level as you have learned to do, and apply the techniques exactly as we have instructed you to. In an emergency, do what you need to do and expect the best. That's what Hector Chacon did when he found himself losing a golf match.

In 1989, Hector Chacon attended the Silva Method course in hopes of finding a way to lift the basketball team he coached out of a slump. He taught his players how to enter the alpha level and program, and they won the bi-district championship.

The Silva Method also helped him with his golf game.

He had only completed half of the Silva course, and when he came for the start of the second half, he asked, "Can you go to level while you are walking?"

"Why do you ask?" his instructor asked him.

"Well, I was playing golf. The first three holes, my partner and I either lost or halved. So when I got back in the golf cart I closed my eyes to go to level. But the others in the foursome all started teasing me."

"So what did you do?"

"I got out of the cart and told them to go on ahead and that I would walk. I lowered my head, tried not to focus my eyes but just sort of daydream and watch where I was going out of the corner of my eye. And I visualized the problem, and then pictured myself winning the next hole."

"And did you?"

"We won every hole."

"Is that normal, that you would win so many holes?"

"No, absolutely not!"

"Then it sounds like you were at your level."

"Do you think so?"

"There's one way to find out: keep programming and see what happens."

He won so much during the next three months that his friends didn't want to continue playing with him. He recommended that if they wanted to have a chance to beat him again, they should take the course!

HELP FROM A HIGHER POWER

In the next chapter, we will teach you the new MentalVideo Technique, which you will use when you go to sleep at night. Prior to going to sleep, you need to review your MentalVideos at the alpha level, so continue your practice of counting yourself into your level.

Your MentalVideos will be delivered to higher intelligence while you sleep, so that your helpers in the spiritual dimension can guide you and help you to achieve your goals.

Meanwhile, here are your two assignments:

1. Use what you have learned in this chapter to correct problems and relieve suffering, in order to make the world a better place to live.

2. Continue to practice with the Silva Centering Exercise or with your countdowns in order to establish a good, deep alpha level from which to function.

Chapter 6
Help From a Higher Power

The MentalVideo Technique is a way for you to communicate with a higher power—what we refer to as *high intelligence*—to find out what your purpose in life is, and how to go about fulfilling your mission.

Anyone can use this technique. You do not need to be a graduate of the Silva UltraMind ESP System, although it helps if you are.

Why is it better to be a Silva graduate? Two reasons:

1. The better able you are to use your inborn psychic ability, the easier it will be to send and receive messages to your helpers in the spiritual dimension.

2. Your ability to do your thinking at the alpha brainwave level—the ideal level for thinking—will help you to better interpret and understand the information that you receive from the other side.

The MentalVideo Technique provides you with a method to give a report of your activities to high intelligence every night. You let your tutors on the other side know what the problems are, and what you are doing to correct them.

Then your tutors send you guidance to help you make the best decisions and proceed in the most efficient and effective manner. Your tutors are part of what my father called the "hierarchy of intelligence" that governs the whole universe. They want to help you to be a big success and will send you all the help you need. Some people think of them as guardian angels.

In order to understand the concept, my father used an analogy about our relationship with higher intelligence.

Your mission

If you're like me, you have probably wondered about the big questions of life, questions like, *Where did I come from? Who sent me here? Why did they send me? What is my purpose? What am I supposed to do while I am here?*

Throughout the years, my research has involved those questions. And I have come up with some answers that stand up to the scrutiny of scientific method. That is, when my findings are applied by myself and by other people, the results are predictable, reliable, and repeatable.

I believe that we were sent here from another dimension, by somebody who had the power to send us here without our consent if they so desired, because I don't remember anybody asking me if I wanted to come.

As for why I was sent here, and what I am supposed to do, my research confirms again and again that we were sent here to correct problems and to convert the earth into a paradise.

Why do I believe this? Because the people who correct the most problems are the people who are the most successful.

What do I mean when I say they are successful?

I am not talking about just making money. To be truly successful, you have to be successful in all areas: health, family, and relationships, and a sense of satisfaction, as well as financial success.

Some of the most successful people have enough money for their needs, but little extra. Look at someone like Gandhi or Mother Theresa; neither had many physical possessions, but they lived long, productive lives and received more satisfaction out of their work than most people can even imagine.

Communication with headquarters

In order to know what to do to fulfill our mission, we need guidance from high intelligence.

All of those who work on the other side—from the highest level of intelligence down to those who are assigned to help us individually, to tutor us—are all spiritual beings, in a spiritual dimension. They don't have physical senses.

Since they don't have physical senses, they cannot detect directly what is taking place in the physical dimension, where we live.

I believe that we were created to function in a physical dimension, to send them information about this dimension, and to carry out the work they want done.

It is like the astronauts who are sent to the moon, or maybe to Mars before long. The astronauts have certain assignments. They know that they are supposed to collect samples.

The reason the scientists need samples is because their knowledge of the moon is limited. So the astronauts call back to headquarters and say, "We found three different kinds of rocks. We will describe them to you, and you tell us what you want us to bring back, how many samples of each."

The astronauts have been trained to fly to the moon and land successfully, and to gather samples, but they do not know the details of what the scientists need or what they will do with the samples. So it is up to the scientists back at NASA headquarters to tell them.

The scientists are not going to get samples unless the astronauts bring them. If the astronauts ignore their mission and decide to do what they please, the scientists will not get the samples they need. And if the astronauts are not able to get information from the scientists about what to collect, their mission might be only partially successful, or not at all.

The scientists back at NASA headquarters cannot see what the astronauts see, because the scientists are not in that environment. The astronauts are.

Getting the guidance we need

This parallels our situation.

We are in a physical environment. We report back to high intelligence, to headquarters.

Headquarters then determines what they need, and lets us carry it out, just like the scientists at NASA headquarters determine what they need in order to conduct their research, and then convey the information to the astronauts on the moon, so that the astronauts can carry out the instructions and complete their mission successfully.

It is up to the astronauts to determine how to move around, where to go to avoid obstacles and move towards their goal. The scientists are too far away to tell them every detail, like stepping around this boulder and picking up that rock.

How to best do our job

In the same way, the details of how to carry out our assignment are up to us. It is our choice whether to accept our assignment or not, and how to carry it out.

The better you are at detecting information psychically with your mental senses, as well as detecting information physically with your physical senses, and then analyzing at the alpha level, the greater your chances of achieving complete success.

It takes a cooperative effort to have a successful mission. If the astronauts just go up there and do nothing but hit golf balls, and do not bring back the samples that the scientists at headquarters need, the mission will be a failure. They can have a little fun hitting a couple of balls, as long as they carry out the mission that has been assigned to them.

If the astronauts do not receive the proper instructions and guidance from the scientists at headquarters, and if they are not given all of the tools and training that they need to do the job that's been assigned to them, the mission will be a failure.

So the scientists and engineers at headquarters provide the spacecraft and the appropriate tools for this particular mission, and they train the astronauts so that they have the knowledge and skills that are required, and then they send them into space, into another environment, fully equipped to succeed at the mission that the scientists have established for them.

If the astronauts try to change their mission's objectives, their mission will be a failure.

If they do not maintain communication to get the guidance they need, their mission will fail.

If they do not use their own judgment—as the people who are actually on the scene—to overcome obstacles, their mission will fail.

They have free will to do what is necessary to complete their mission successfully, based on the guidance from headquarters.

They also have the free will to disregard the instructions and fail if they so choose.

You are fully equipped for success

We have been equipped with bodies suitable for the physical dimension, and have been sent here to accomplish certain objectives.

I believe that each one of us has been given all of the tools, talent, and training that we need to accomplish the mission we were sent here to do.

People who select their own goals, and then fail, disregard the mission that was given to them. If they had used their given abilities for the mission that was assigned to them, they would have succeeded.

Some people say that we have been given everything we need to succeed at anything we want to do. My research indicates otherwise: that we have been given everything we need to succeed at the mission that has been assigned to us, the mission that we were sent here to do.

YOU ARE CONNECTED TO THE SOURCE

One of the best Silva lecturers we ever had was Paul Grivas in New York City. He said, "You are to God what your fingers are to your hand." That is a good example. Your mind conceives an idea, your brain processes the information, and your fingers do the work.

Higher intelligence makes the plan (on earth as it is in heaven—it all starts in the heavenly dimension), we process the information mentally at our center, the alpha brain-wave level, and then we get our body into motion and go do the work that needs to be done in the physical dimension.

As my father said, our assignment is to correct problems, complete the creation of the planet, and convert our planet into a paradise.

COMMUNICATION WITH HIGHER INTELLIGENCE

Now let's take a look at the practical side of things, the specific ways that we can establish and maintain contact with "headquarters" in the spiritual dimension.

The MentalVideo Technique is an outstanding way to send reports of what you are doing and what you intend to do back to headquarters in the spiritual dimension.

However, another system is required for receiving information back from them. Let's talk about that for a moment.

The second best way to receive guidance from higher intelligence is through thoughts—dreams, inspiration, and ideas you get while at alpha, and so forth.

The problem is, sometimes we want things so badly that we think that our own thoughts, our own fantasies, are actually messages from God. And sometimes we just plain misunderstand the ideas and instructions that are sent to us mentally. Therefore, the more practice you have detecting information psychically and analyzing information at the alpha level, the better you will be at interpreting correctly.

PRAYING FOR HELP

There is a story about the time it rained so much that a river overflowed its banks. To make sure everyone knew there was danger and they should evacuate, the sheriff's department sent a deputy around to warn residents.

When they got to Farmer Brown's house, he told the deputy that he had faith in the Lord, and that he would pray and would be okay.

The deputy did not have time to stay and argue, for there were many other people who needed to be warned.

Sure enough, the waters rose, and soon Farmer Brown had fled to the second floor of his house. He looked out the window and saw a boat from the Marine Patrol. The officer called to him to get into the boat, but Farmer Brown, his strong faith undaunted, declined the offer, saying, "I'll trust in God to take care of me."

When the waters had risen so high that Farmer Brown had been forced to climb to the very top of his roof, he heard a loud clattering and looked up to see a helicopter from the Air National Guard. "Grab the rope," they yelled down, "and we'll lift you to safety."

Again, Farmer Brown declined the offer.

A little while later, as Farmer Brown appeared at the gates of Heaven, St. Peter greeted him. "You have been such a devoted and faithful servant," St. Peter said, "would you like to meet the Lord?"

After he was ushered in, God asked Farmer Brown if he had any questions.

"Well, I do have one," Farmer Brown answered. "I always believed that you would protect me and take care of me. Why did you let me drown, instead of keeping me safe?"

"What do you mean?" God answered. "I sent a car to get you out. When I checked back and saw that you were still there, I sent the Marine

Patrol by with a boat. When I saw that you had missed the boat, I even arranged for a helicopter to come get you and take you to safety!"

RECOGNIZING HELP WHEN IT COMES

If Farmer Brown had known how to use the alpha level to analyze the situation, he might have figured out what was happening. Good intuition—the ability to detect information—certainly would have been valuable to him.

High intelligence is spiritual, in a spiritual dimension. Spiritual beings do not have vocal cords to talk to us. They communicate with us through mental projection and through coincidence.

In order to ensure that you do not confuse your own fantasies and desires with the guidance and instructions from your tutors in the spiritual dimension, you need to have a way to test the information and verify it.

How do you verify it? How do you determine that it was mental projection from your tutors and not your own fantasies?

By acting on the information and ideas and observing the results.

If you pray for help, and help arrives, take it! Farmer Brown would have been much better off if he had understood this.

ACTION SPEAKS LOUDER THAN WORDS

It is always better to evaluate people by what they do, not what they say.

We live in a physical world; tangible results are what count.

My father adopted this philosophy in his studies and research. He read so many books that made so many claims, which were often conflicting, that he had to develop a system to evaluate the ideas and information from those authors.

To test the value of the ideas in the books, he put them into action by trying them out. If they corrected problems, he considered them to be real.

He said it this way: "The truthful truth, and the real reality, is that which, when applied, corrects problems."

The same thing works for evaluating the guidance you think you are getting from high intelligence.

Try it out. Use it. Apply it. And then notice what happens within the next two or three days. If, after you act on the information, something positive happens—something that moves you toward your goals—this is an indication that you could be on the right track.

If, on the other hand, you encounter new obstacles after you apply the information you receive, this is an indication that you could be headed in the wrong direction.

A FORMULA FOR EVALUATING IDEAS

My father explained it this way:

As you work on your project, you will usually encounter obstacles. Notice how long it takes you to overcome the first obstacle. Then when you encounter a second obstacle, notice how long it takes you to overcome this second obstacle.

If it takes twice as long to overcome the second obstacle as it did the first, then this might indicate that you are moving in the wrong direction. But we are not yet sure. We do not want to give up too soon.

So you continue. When you encounter a third obstacle, notice how long it takes to overcome the third obstacle.

If it takes twice as long to overcome the third obstacle as it did to overcome the second, and it took twice as long to overcome the second obstacle as it did the first, then you can be pretty sure that you are going in the wrong direction.

However, if it only takes half as long to overcome the second obstacle as it did to overcome the first, and just half as long to overcome the third as it took for the second, then you can be pretty confident that you are moving in the correct direction. Keep going, full speed ahead.

Remember, we do not batter down doors. If a door doesn't open for you, and you have made a good effort to open it, then back up and take another look. There might be another door that will open right up for you. That is the door to take.

And as former Silva instructor Marie Burleson pointed out, "When you stop struggling and back up to survey the situation, you might find that the door you were pushing on actually opens toward you!"

A WRONG INTERPRETATION IS CORRECTED

After my father had been conducting research for about a decade, he began to feel that maybe he had done enough, that it was time to bring his research to an end.

There were several reasons he felt this way:

1. He had used hypnosis to learn more about how the brain and mind work in order to help my sisters and brothers make better grades.

2. His research had even helped him to develop specific techniques to correct additional problems. What more could he need?

3. He had been neglecting his radio- and television-repair business. He was spending his own money on his research instead of on his family.

4. He was traveling quite a bit and was spending a lot of time away from his family and his business.

5. And, one of the most troubling things to him personally: he was receiving a lot of criticism. Friends thought he was a witch doctor because of his holistic faith-healing research; he was an excellent holistic faith-healer. Even his church was critical because they didn't know what he was delving into, and they feared for his "soul."

So one rainy Saturday morning, it all came to a head. He decided to end his research. He put his psychology books into boxes and climbed up to the attic to store them away. He recalled the story this way:

A decision to quit

I had written to Dr. J.B. Rhine to tell him that I had trained my daughter Isabel to be a psychic. But Dr. Rhine, a leading parapsychology researcher, wrote and told me that ESP could not be taught, and that my daughter was probably a "natural" psychic. He pointed out that I had not "pretested" her to make sure she was not already a psychic.

I figured the number-one man in parapsychology was saying it, so it must be right. But the thought of starting all over again with a new subject that I must pretest first was just too much for me. It had taken three years to get where I was, and that turned out to be a big zero, according to Dr. Rhine.

It was with these bleak thoughts on a dismal, cloudy Saturday morning that I decided to quit this nonsense. So I put my books in the attic and sat on the sofa in my living room, thinking.

My mind reached back into the memories, the feelings associated with the research I had done to that point, the research that now had come to a dead end.

Although he was disappointed, he had learned to pay attention to the "coincidences" that high intelligence sends to us to let us know how to proceed.

Although he didn't realize it, he was about to be told that he had misinterpreted the situation.

An unexpected messenger

Suddenly Ricardo, my second son, who was almost 10 years old, came bursting through the front door and interrupted my thoughts.

It had been raining and was still drizzling outside. Ricardo was soaked, but the roll of heavy paper he dropped on the table was dry!

When I unrolled that paper, I got the surprise of my life: Christ was staring at me!

It was a picture of Christ's face, as large as life, looking at me with dark piercing eyes, not judging, but full of love and compassion, and I felt as though He was asking, "Why did you stop studying? Did I not tell you to study psychology?"

Tears came to my eyes and a feeling as though I had been a bad boy for not obeying.

I swore then that I would continue with this work, and not ever again stop for the rest of my life, even if it meant giving up on my very successful electronics business.

MANY COINCIDENCES

It was a prior "coincidence" that triggered so much emotion in my father. The first time he encountered the field of psychology was when he was interviewed by two psychiatrists when he was inducted into the army in 1944. During that same induction process he was given a picture of Christ, which was something familiar in that strange environment farther from his home than he had ever been before. As a result, he always associated his study of psychology with Christ.

True to his word, he never stopped his research after getting that message via the picture of Christ. The picture still hangs inside the entrance to Silva International Headquarters in Laredo, Texas, along with a photograph of my father looking at the original, a full-length painting of Jesus with a child standing by His side, painted by Carl Heinrich Bloch, which now hangs in a church in Denmark.

Let's review and see just what happened: My father always had a strong connection with high intelligence, as evidenced by his success his entire life. Relaxing on the sofa on a Saturday morning while a gentle rain fell outside is a perfect prescription for this natural alpha thinker to be at alpha, a condition where communication with high intelligence is very easy.

Evidently, his tutor observed that he had interpreted the criticism of him and his work as a sign to end his research.

But, as he came to understand later, more formidable criticism from skeptical scientists lay ahead that he would have to contend with if he hoped to have his work accepted. The criticism of his nonscientific friends and neighbors strengthened him, and it showed him how to deal with resistance and opposition.

So how did high intelligence get this message to him?

By using a symbol that he could understand.

They got his attention through the strange circumstances surrounding the picture—the papers were dry.

And what did Jesus represent to my father? Someone who endured criticism and suffering in order to help humanity.

He got the message. His emotions were so overwhelming that he went into the bathroom, locked the door, and had a good cry.

Proceeding with the MentalVideo Technique

The MentalVideo Technique is the first technique that uses the delta brain-wave level. Until now, nobody knew how to use the delta level, because the only way most people can get to the delta level is in the deepest part of their sleep cycles.

Here are the steps for guidance from higher intelligence:

1. Follow the instructions in this section for creating the MentalVideos at beta and alpha levels.

2. When you go to sleep at night, use the technique to deliver your MentalVideos to your tutor in order to give a full report to higher intelligence while you are in delta sleep.

3. Let "coincidence" and the results of your efforts guide you to correct problems and reach your goals.

Specific examples

First, before we use the MentalVideo, you need to gather and analyze some information. If you have not yet found your purpose in life, your first step is to analyze and find out what your tendencies are.

What made you happy when you were young? What were your dreams? Why were they important to you?

What has brought you the most satisfaction in your life? What do you seem to be good at? What do your friends think you are good at? What do they think you are well suited for?

Questions such as these can help you find a starting point.

Then, use the MentalVideo Technique, and get into action.

Start working toward what you think your purpose in life might be. Notice how it goes: Do you encounter many obstacles, and each one takes longer to overcome than the previous one? You might be on the wrong path. Try again.

If each obstacle seems less difficult to overcome than the previous one, and if coincidences are making it easy for you to move toward your goals, you are probably on the right path. Keep going!

Whenever you need to make decisions, use your level—the alpha level—to help you make the best decision you can. Deliver your MentalVideo while in delta sleep, and the next day notice the results of your action. This will let you know whether or not you actually made the correct decision.

As long as you continue to give reports to the director back at headquarters in the spiritual dimension, the director will arrange things to either help you or to redirect your efforts, whichever helps to accomplish what needs to be accomplished to conform to the plan of high intelligence for this physical dimension.

Remember, you are the eyes and ears for higher intelligence. Higher intelligence needs your reports, so be sure to report in every night.

Then, whenever you try something and it works, keep doing it. If it doesn't work, do something else. Don't give up too easily—make a good effort. Just remember that we do not batter down doors. We do whatever is the best, most efficient way to reach our goals. Or if we keep getting blocked, we change our goals.

It is such a simple system that it is easy to ignore it. Give regular reports. Then do what works, and avoid what doesn't work.

MENTALVIDEO TECHNIQUE

Whenever you need to solve a problem with the MentalVideo Technique, proceed as follows:

1. At beta, the outer-conscious level, analyze your problem. Make a good study of the problem. Imagine that you have a video camera and that you are making a video recording of the problem. Make sure that your video explains the details of the problem.

2. Later, when you are in bed and ready to go to sleep, enter level one with the 3-to-1 method. (See page 41.)

3. Once you are at your level, review the MentalVideo that you created of the problem when you were at the beta level.

4. After you have reviewed the problem, mentally convert the problem into a project. Then create with imagination a MentalVideo of the solution. The MentalVideo of the solution should contain a step-by-step procedure of how you desire the project to be resolved, and what you expect to happen.

5. After both of the MentalVideos have been completed, go to sleep with the intention of delivering the MentalVideos to your tutor while you sleep. Take for granted that delivery will be made.

6. During the next three days, look for indications that point to the solution. Every time you think of the project, think of the solution that you have created in the MentalVideo in a past-tense sense.

Your videos should include everything that has life. We can only influence life. And we definitely *can* influence life: humans, animals, plants, and so forth. Researcher Cleve Backster has demonstrated that plants—and even your own white blood cells—can perceive our thoughts and emotions, even at great distances. You can read about this research in Chapter 8.

In your second video, include all of the people who will benefit. The more people who will benefit, the more help you will get from the other side. At least two or more people should benefit. The solution should improve conditions on planet earth.

The following Laws of Programming are to be considered:

1. Do to others *only* what you like others to do to you.

2. The solution must help to make this planet a better place to live.

3. The solution must be the best for everybody concerned.

4. The solution must help at least two or more persons.

5. The solution must be within the possibility area.

When you use the MentalVideo Technique, do it with the expectation that while you are in delta sleep, the videos will be delivered into the proper hands—the correct intelligence, your tutor—on the other side, to help in the preparation of the solution.

The more that your tutors in the spiritual dimension know about conditions and what is being done to improve them, the better able they will be to arrange things so that we get the help that we need. That is why it is important that as many people as possible are using the MentalVideo Technique every night.

Remember, after you review your MentalVideos, remain at alpha and go to sleep from there, with the intention of delivering them to the other side while you are in delta sleep.

USING DELTA PURPOSEFULLY

Why does this delivery take place at the delta level?

We have observed that delta is like a doorway to the other side. The first brain frequencies ever detected in the fetus are the slow delta frequencies. After birth, the child first develops the delta dimension, then theta, alpha, and beta by the time the person is fully mature.

When a person dies a natural death, the last frequencies detected are the delta frequencies. This Delta Doorway seems to bring us from another dimension into the physical dimension and then take us back to the spiritual dimension again.

The only way that most people can get to delta is by natural sleep. If you take sleeping pills, the pills interfere with your normal sleep rhythms, and often keep you out of delta. Drugs always have side effects. It is much better to learn the Silva Sleep Control Technique to get to sleep without drugs.

USING THE MENTALVIDEO TECHNIQUE FOR MANY PROJECTS

You can the MentalVideo Technique for several projects.

As always, let your results guide you as to how to proceed.

When you first begin, do just one project at a time. After this becomes successful for you, then you can try two projects at a time. You can continue adding projects as you feel necessary, always observing the results.

If your success rate declines, then go back to including fewer projects in your MentalVideos. If your success rate remains high, then continue on.

As always, do what works, and avoid what doesn't work.

CONVERTING PROBLEMS INTO PROJECTS

Several people have asked what we mean by converting a problem into a project. We explain it this way in class: It is only a problem when you don't know what to do about it. Once you are working on the solution, it is no longer a problem; it is a project.

Usually it is easier to explain things with examples of actual projects on which you are working. For instance, if I want a promotion at my workplace, I would make a video depicting me in my current job, improving my skills so that I am qualified for the new job, submitting the application or talking with my supervisor about it, getting the word that I've gotten the promotion, and then enjoying the new job. These can be quick shots of each step, the way you see in television programs. Do whatever you think it takes to get the idea across. Involve your feelings: *What would it feel like if...?*

If you don't know the steps involved, just depict whatever you can. Imagine you are making an actual, physical video to submit to somebody with the power to help you reach that goal. What would you need to show this person? Imagery is the universal language, so it is the pictures that count, not something you might say. So you want to imagine a video with a picture of each step, or the steps you think are necessary for higher intelligence to understand what you are working on, what you think will be the best way to get there, and the desired end result.

Also remember the Laws of Programming, and when you get to the end result, depict all of the people who will benefit. One reason people fail to get results with MentalVideo is that their project does not conform to all of the Laws of Programming. They might be trying to take a job away from someone else who is also qualified to have that job, which would not be the best thing for everyone concerned.

My father also advised us that we do not want to gain at somebody else's loss. So our project would have to take into account what will happen to the person we will replace: Will that person get an even better job? Of course, if that person is not doing a good job, then there are other people who will benefit when you take over and do a better job.

If you don't see any "indications" within three days, there could be several reasons. As mentioned previously, review the Laws of Programming. Also, at your level, review the things that have happened during the last three days and think about whether any of them could be an indication. If you think that something might have been an indication of how to proceed, but you are not quite sure, then you can do another MentalVideo and get confirmation. One of two things will happen:

Something will come along to confirm the first "indication," or you will get an indication that the first was not an indication, or that you interpreted it incorrectly.

It takes a little while to get used to it. Once you do, you will catch on very quickly. Sometimes the indications are very subtle. Almost every time I use the MentalVideo, the same thing happens: The next day I get a call from somebody, or I hear something on the radio, or an idea occurs to me, and I act on it and something good comes from it, or somebody comes by to see me, or someone tells me about something that is happening in his or her life that gives me an idea—all of which are physical things. And whatever it is that happens, it helps me, and I feel very good about it. Then, after a while, I realize: *Oh, I did the MentalVideo last night, that was my "indication."* It didn't happen because of something I did; it was guidance from higher intelligence.

SEEKING GUIDANCE DIFFERS FROM PROGRAMMING

The difference between the MentalVideo and the 3-Scenes Technique is that with the 3-Scenes Technique, you are just using your mind in the subjective (mental) dimension to influence things here on planet earth. You can influence your boss to give you the promotion, whether it is the best thing for you or not. My father included a story in *Sales Power* (Putnam Publishing Group, 1992) about a lady who programmed a certain man to marry her. "You can do this," she told us, "it works, I know. But," she added, "it might not be the right thing for you." It sure wasn't for her. When they got divorced a few years later, he ended up with the real estate business that she founded, and she ended up with a better understanding of things.

The time to use the 3-Scenes Technique is when you have received guidance from higher intelligence, and confirmed it if you feel the need. Then, when you are sure that higher intelligence has confirmed that you are the right person for the job, use the 3-Scenes Technique to help you prepare for your meeting with your supervisor. I would program myself to make an appropriate presentation, one that will produce the result that is the best for all concerned, the result that higher intelligence wants. I have always included the statements: "May God's will be done," and, "May the best thing be done for everybody concerned." In the third scene I picture myself successful in the project, but I keep in mind that higher intelligence might have another idea, and I am okay with that if it happens.

If you program that way, you may not achieve as many of your projects with the 3-Scenes Technique, but you will probably live a better life. If the real estate lady had programmed that the solution be the best for everybody concerned, then maybe she would not have succeeded in getting that man to marry her, and thus would not have lost everything in the divorce a few years later.

If you don't know what the solution (or the desired outcome) is, you cannot use the 3-Scenes Technique. But you can use the MentalVideo: In your video, depict yourself perplexed as to what you should do, and expect to receive an indication from higher intelligence to guide you.

My father's idea was that it is not up to us to make that final decision. We should do what we believe is right, what we think is the best thing, and we should be open to guidance from higher intelligence.

You can think of it like working on a job. Your supervisor tells you to do something, such as rearrange the furniture or write a letter. You get to work on it. Later, when the supervisor looks in to see how you are doing, she says that she would prefer the desk over there instead of where you moved it, or that this paragraph would not be good to include, so please take it out.

In other words, she will praise the things you do right, and she will let you know the things that could be improved.

Higher intelligence will do the same for you, as long as you are using the MentalVideo to keep higher intelligence advised of what you are doing and what the results are.

It is not about us doing what we want. It is about us doing what higher intelligence wants us to do.

Not "my" will, but "Thy will be done, on earth as it is in heaven." In other words, my father pointed out, the plans are already made in heaven, now it is up to us to carry them out here on planet earth.

JOSE SILVA'S FAVORITE FORMULA

My father's favorite formula was:

"Seek ye first the kingdom of heaven and function within God's righteousness, then all else will be added unto you."

He interpreted the "kingdom of heaven" to be the alpha level, an inner kingdom that you reach by becoming similar to a child—brain-wise. Function at 10 cycles alpha, which is the overall predominate brain frequency of a 10-year-old child.

You can "function within God's righteousness" by using the MentalVideo to discover what higher intelligence wants you to do and which problems it wants you to work on, and how to go about solving them and correcting abnormalities.

Then, as a result of doing this, "all else will be added unto you."

Too may people do it the opposite way. They promise that if they have good fortune, they will share it with others. They tithe (give 10 percent of their incomes to the church). They call our office and tell us that if we will tell them how to pick the winning lottery number, they will give half their winnings to charity. We tell them that if we knew how to pick the winning lottery number, we wouldn't tell them—we'd do it ourselves. My father used to say that promises don't count, it is performance that counts.

"What have you done with what you already have?" he would ask people. "Higher intelligence wants to see your track record. How much have you been giving to charity in the past?"

People protest that they cannot give what they do not have. He would point out that we all have something, we can all do something.

This may not sound logical to you at the normal left-brain beta level. When you learn how to reach a deep alpha level, then you will understand.

To help you get started, be sure to review the Laws of Programming from time to time. If you are not getting the results you desire, then go to your level and review the Laws of Programming to see if you are complying with them.

Follow the formula, and all that you need will be added unto you. Thank you.

Chapter 7

Psychometry—ESP in the Palm of Your Hand

Psychometry is an excellent way for you to develop your intuitive ability.

Psychometry is defined as "the ability or art of divining information about people or events associated with an object solely by touching or being near to it."

This is possible because information is stored in matter. Your body is radiating energy through a special field called the aura.

The physical part of your aura extends approximately 8 meters (25 feet) from your body, and affects whatever it comes into contact with. This physical energy can be measured by objective instruments, outside of your body, such as the way the electroencephalograph measures brain activity.

In addition to being absorbed by matter, information is also reflected from matter. Let's take a close look at what happens.

When light strikes a piece of metal, some of the light is absorbed (in the form of heat) and some is reflected from it. What you see from the outside is what is reflected. You cannot see what is absorbed. You can feel the heat that is absorbed. When an object is within range of the physical part of your aura, then information about you is stored in the object. If you take an object that has been in someone's possession for a while, you can detect information about the person, information that is stored in the object.

The easiest way to do this is to hold the object in your left hand and enter your level. Project your mind into the object—do not wait to "perceive" information—and start thinking about what kind of person the object belonged to, what that person might have looked like, and what his or her personality might have been like.

Did it belong to a male or a female? Think of a male, think of a female. You will get a sense about which is correct. Is this person young or old? Think of both, and you will get a sense about which is correct. This is an excellent way to develop your intuition.

When you have developed your skill and your confidence with psychometry, you can use it to locate missing persons, for instance. Once you get a sense of the person, you can imagine seeing through his or her eyes; you can look around and see where you are, and then you will know where the missing person is.

THE SCIENCE BEHIND PSYCHOMETRY

To gain a better understanding of how psychometry works, let's look into how things around us work. The following was written by my father:

Everything that exists vibrates. Everything that exists has a fundamental frequency. The frequency is determined by the composition of the elements in the atoms, and the atoms in the molecules.

The total sum of atoms in a specific type of matter determines the fundamental frequency of that type of matter.

Everything is affected by light.

When light comes into contact with an object, we have the fundamental frequency of the object, and we have the fundamental frequency of light. When the two collide, we end up with four frequencies:

1. The fundamental frequency of the object.

2. The fundamental frequency of light.

3. The sum of the two.

4. The difference of the two.

With our physical senses we are able to detect the difference of the two, which is reflected.

The sum of the two is what is absorbed. We are able to detect what is absorbed with our subjective senses, our intuitive senses.

What is reflected is affected by other reflections, by other energies.

What is absorbed is pure.

Now what do you think is the best information for you to sense:

Information with your physical senses, or information with your subjective senses?

The information that is absorbed is pure.

The information that is absorbed is the information that you would like to use to help you in decision-making.

Now we know that everything vibrates.

We sense information from the vibrations of an object.

The vibrations from your aura—the various energies that radiate from your brain and body—penetrate objects within your presence, and affect the internal vibrations of objects within your aura range.

Your body radiation charges up the objects with your own frequencies.

When you touch a ring, for instance, your vibrations penetrate the ring and it becomes an extension of you.

Anytime later, when someone touches the ring, and desires to obtain information, that person can obtain information from those vibrations in the ring.

The vibrations in an object are used by our mind to help us tune in to the person. Whenever we desire to obtain information on that person, it will be helpful if we have an object from that person. When we sense the vibrations within that object, that will help our mind to be able to tune in to that person to obtain the information that we need.

HOW TO PRACTICE PSYCHOMETRY

You can use psychometry to help you develop your intuitive ability.

As you learn to function in the alpha level, you can have friends or family members bring you objects from people they know, and give you a description of the people: The color of their hair and eyes, their complexion, and maybe their height and weight.

Hold the object in the palm of your left hand and decide what information you would like to detect. Then, enter your level and desire to detect that information.

Usually the information that you perceive immediately is the correct information.

Once you finish, compare your answers with the information that was provided to you.

This will help you to gain confidence, and to establish points of reference that you are doing the right thing.

On average, an untrained person, when guessing, will be correct one out of five times.

On average, a good psychic will be correct four out of five times.

Once you have determined that you are correct more than one out of five times, then you are on your way to developing better intuition.

THE TRUTH IS WITHIN US

Which is the more accurate information: That which is reflected by the object, and you can detect with your objective senses? Or that which is absorbed, which you can detect with your subjective senses?

We are always transmitting energy through our auras. Some of that energy is reflected off of objects in the vicinity, and then contacts other people in the environment.

Some of the energy is absorbed by the object, and is stored there. It makes changes to the object, and later you can use your subjective senses to detect that information.

When you desire to detect information that is stored in an object, you can detect it—you *will* detect it.

Your desire is a tuning mechanism that will cause your mind to tune to the information that you desire to detect...that you have a need to detect. You can detect information about any one specific person out of all of the thousands of people who have transmitted energy into the object—by tuning in with your desire, backed up by a need to have the information.

You can begin learning how to detect information by practicing psychometry. As you gain experience and confidence, you will then be able to detect any information that you need to correct a problem and improve conditions on the planet directly with your mind without having to hold an object in your hand.

PROGRAMMING WITH PSYCHOMETRY

We are affected by everything in our environment, even though we may not be consciously aware of it at the time. It takes practice to learn to detect information with psychometry and to become consciously aware of the information.

You can protect yourself from negative influences in the environment by occasionally reminding yourself, while at your level, that "Negative thoughts and negative suggestions have no effect on me at any level of the mind."

The more you develop your Everyday ESP, the more aware you will be of both negative and positive influences in the environment.

It is a good idea to stay away from negative people, and even to avoid being in the environment where negative people have been.

My father used to say that if you want to develop certain characteristics, then use objects that belonged to people who had those characteristics. As an example, he mentioned how most people will give brand-new items to a newly married couple, including dishes and cooking utensils. He said it would be better to give them cooking utensils that had been used by an excellent cook for many years. Those utensils would have the energy of that person stored within them, and this energy would influence the novice cook.

Those "good vibrations" will also be transmitted to the food. In fact, the mood of the person preparing the food will be transmitted to the food also, so please keep that in mind when you are preparing food for your family, and think the kind of thoughts that will help, support, and encourage your family members.

The same applies to tools that a carpenter or mechanic uses. Tools that have been used by an excellent carpenter or mechanic will help you to do a better job.

While it takes practice to develop proficiency in detecting information, everyone can and does project information into everything within the aura range.

Because you are doing that naturally anyway, it is easy for you to "charge" an object with a program that can help someone.

JoNell Monaco Lytle, a long-time Silva instructor in Virginia Beach, Virginia, has used this method of programming very effectively. She had a relative who wanted to stop smoking, so she went to his house and programmed objects in every room to help him stop smoking.

You can use the 3-Scenes Technique that we covered in Chapter 5 to do this. First enter your level. Then strengthen your desire to help the person by thinking of all the benefits when he stops smoking—how the individual will benefit, how the person's loved ones will benefit, how the person's employer will benefit, and so on. This will make your programming more effective.

Then, in the first scene, use visualization by recalling a time when you saw the person smoking. Then shift your attention toward your left, to the second scene, and use imagination to envision the person starting to reach for a cigarette (which is what you are programming for), and then having the urge not to smoke the cigarette, and in fact not smoking the cigarette.

You know the person, so use your imagination any way that seems appropriate to you to picture his desire to smoke lessening over time. You will spend more time in the second scene than either of the other two scenes. When you feel that you have done a good job in the second scene, then shirt your attention still further to your left and, in the third scene, imagine the person being a nonsmoker and very happy with his accomplishment.

In the future, whenever you think of the project (it is no longer a "problem" now that you are working on it, it is a "project"), visualize the image that you created in the third scene of the person as a nonsmoker. If you see the person smoking, or think about the person smoking, just "cancel" that image and recall (visualize) the image of the person as a nonsmoker.

Psychometry in Depth

For the technically inclined, here is an in-depth look at psychometry, followed by some specific ways it can help you, written by my father:

Vibrations are related to, and depend on, the light of the sun.

Anything that produces light is a transmitter. It produces light energy. Light is energy.

The complete spectrum of energy covers all the vibrations that the body responds to, or has within it.

The visual spectrum is a complete spectrum which, when complete, produces white light. It goes from the red up to the violet. This is what we can perceive with our senses.

Each of the vibrations of our senses responds and combines with specific frequencies. It detects and vibrates with these frequencies. It is repels some of these frequencies, and it absorbs some of these frequencies.

When your sensing faculty detects a frequency, some of it is absorbed and some is repelled. The frequency that is absorbed is converted to a different frequency, which is then transmitted to the brain.

All senses receive energy from the electromagnetic spectrum, convert it to nerve energy, and transmit it to the brain.

The sense of sight receives light energy, converts it to nerve energy, and transmits it to the brain.

The same can be said of the senses of smell, taste, touch, and hearing.

Our biological senses detect physical vibrations, convert them, and transmit them to the left brain hemisphere.

The brain receives nerve energy from the physical senses, converts it to subjective energy, and transmits it to the right brain hemisphere.

The right brain hemisphere also has a set of senses. They are subjective, at a different dimension, not within the physical electromagnetic spectrum that includes sound vibrations, visible light, and so on.

We have two different things happening that we need to interpret:

When we talk about matter, matter is a composition of atomic structure. The vibration of the atomic structure of a particular type of matter depends on the distance of electrons that are circling around the nucleus, or heart, of the atom.

The number of atoms, and their distance from the nucleus, and the rate of circling around the nucleus, produces the rate of vibration.

The sum total of all atoms of a specific type of matter is the fundamental frequency of that type of matter.

All inanimate matter—the mineral world—has these vibrations.

When your sense of sight detects vibration from matter, your senses detect what is reflected by the object.

Your biological senses detect what is reflected from the object.

Your subjective senses detect what is absorbed by the object.

Every object has a different rate of vibration because of the different composition of matter—atomic structure.

The object's vibration collides with the vibration of the electromagnetic energy—light, for instance. In the case of light, we now have two fundamentals: the fundamental frequency of the object, and the fundamental of light.

When they come together, they add to one another, so we have the sum of both; and when they collide with each other, one neutralizes some of the other, and we have the difference between the two.

So we have four fundamentals:

○ The object.

○ Light.

○ The sum of both.

○ The difference between them.

It is like a frequency multiplier, or divider, that can reduce the frequency from a very high rate, to a rate that the senses can perceive.

Take the eye for instance:

○ The eye has its own radiating vibration.

○ The reflected object has its own.

Now when light strikes the object, the difference between the fundamental frequency of the object and the fundamental frequency of the light will reflect and be detected by the eye.

When the difference between the object and the light collides with the eye, it interacts with the fundamental of the eye, and the difference is detected by the eye, converted to nerve energy, and transmitted to the brain.

Each sense does the same thing.

Everything has to do with vibrations—sense of touch, sense of smell, all of them.

Now the right brain hemisphere is connected to the subjective senses.

The subjective senses detect subjective information, the vibrations that are absorbed by the object.

The left brain hemisphere detects information that is reflected by the object.

The right brain hemisphere detects what is absorbed by the object.

Now which of the two would you say would be the most accurate information about the object: What is reflected from it, or what is absorbed?

What's absorbed is not distorted by anything.

What's reflected can be distorted by other reflections.

There are many other reflections that can contaminate the reflection from the object—the reflection that is detected by the physical senses.

But there is nothing to distort or contaminate the inner vibrations that are detected by the subjective senses and transmitted to the right brain hemisphere.

So the right brain hemisphere, the subjective senses, detects things more accurately.

Your thought—your mind—is what locks in on something and detects it.

At alpha, you can detect the object from within. At beta, you can only detect what is reflected from it.

Being within, because there is no "law of physics" involved, it is as though everything is together.

Your thoughts are the tuning mechanism to change from one frequency to another.

When you are thinking about a typewriter, for instance, you adjust yourself to the vibrating rate of the atomic structure that is absorbed by the typewriter. When you picture it in your mind and think about it, you are there already.

With the physical senses, you have to get it objectively. If you are not there, you have to go where it is in order to detect information about it.

But when you visualize it in your mind, at the alpha level, you are already there. You can describe it from within, just as you can describe it from the outside.

This is beyond physics. Metaphysics.

That's the fourth dimension.

In physics you have the height, width, length. The fourth dimension is the depth—the inner dimension that you can detect only with your mind. Penetrating matter and detecting information from the inside.

We say that spiritual medicine operates from within the inner layers of matter, to the outer layers of matter.

Physical medicine operates, or helps, from the outer layers to the inner layers of matter.

Now we can help from both ends: from within, or from without, to solve the problem much faster.

Neither one covers everything. We need both of them. It is like saying, "I need the sense of sight, and the sense of hearing also." Not just one. It depends on what is required—whether you need to see or need to hear.

We cannot hear at the frequency of sight, and cannot see at the frequency of hearing. We need different channels in order to do both.

The same thing now with left and right brain hemisphere: we have to attune to them, and use the appropriate one, depending on what is required to correct a problem. They operate on two different bands—they are two different ways of communicating, similar to a.m. radio and f.m. radio. You cannot hear a.m. stations on the f.m. band, and you cannot hear f.m. stations on the a.m. band. You have to tune to the correct one.

To learn everything about matter, you need to use both bands: one external, the other internal. One objective, the other subjective. One left brain, the other right brain.

We need to train our mind to do this.

Healing subjectively

When it comes to correcting problems subjectively, inanimate matter is one thing, animate matter is another.

With inanimate matter, the law of physics takes over. There are a lot of things that cannot be done to inanimate matter except through the laws of physics—through physical means:

If you want to move something, you move it physically.

Right brain thinking—subjective thinking—imagination—has an energy to cause life to move. Not inanimate matter, though.

But animate matter will follow a blueprint that you create with your mind.

If a plant is not producing what it should, you imagine it producing it. You are going to help it do what it is supposed to do. You cannot get the plant to do something it is not supposed to do.

You cannot get an apple tree to produce oranges; that is impossible, because that does not conform to the original blueprint. But you can help it produce more apples.

Objectively, you can hurt an apple tree and cause it to produce fewer apples, or more apples.

Subjectively, you can help it produce more apples, but you cannot change the normal to the abnormal, to produce fewer apples.

You can only influence, subjectively, within, what the plant is supposed to do, not what it is unable to do.

If the plant is supposed to produce, it is going to produce. You cannot get it to not produce through subjective means.

With the left brain hemisphere, you can help or you can hurt. You can help it to produce more, or keep it from producing. You can hurt it or you can help it through objective means.

Subjectively, you can never hurt anything. You can only help it to do what it is supposed to do.

The subjective, right brain energy, controls the creative process. In order to create something, you need to first have a blueprint. You create the blueprint with imagination, then matter will conform to the image that you have in your mind. But you must have animate matter; you cannot do it with inanimate matter, because it has no intelligence.

Inanimate matter cannot move, because there are no cells there, no life. Animate matter can move toward perfection, toward the original blueprint.

Imagination has the power to correct problems with animate matter. But it has to be done with the right brain, with subjective energy.

It could be that the person developed a bad habit that damaged part of his or her body, the heart, for instance. Or it could be that somebody along the way made a mistake—papa or mama, for instance, in conceiving, or because they had a health problem while conceiving and it was transferred to the child. Now we have to correct it.

Relationships

Husband and wife need to have the same vibrations in order to get along.

The vibrations change in the bodies of individuals.

How do you start loving somebody? Or anything?

By changing that person or thing to your vibrations, or to similar vibrations, in order to be alike.

The way it starts is like this:

A boy is walking on one side of the street, and a girl is walking down the other side of the street.

They see each other and they like what they see.

Energy radiates about 8 meters from the body. So if they are within 16 meters of each other (about 50 feet), then their auras are contacting each other.

What are they trying to do?

He is trying to change her aura to be more like his, and she is trying to change his aura to hers.

Their body radiations are different, but when they spend enough time together, they finally match.

There are several stages to contact:

First is sight.

Then the sense of touch.

Voice, and so on.

The closer they get, the stronger the changes.

It is a battle between two auras, trying to change each other.

Finally, kissing, hugging, and the sex act—bingo!—the chemistry is completely changed now.

If either one finds somebody else that they like, and their aura starts changing to be similar to the other person, they start having problems because they don't match anymore. They don't synchronize. There is something about each other that they don't like, and they start having problems.

That's why you should not let yourself become attracted to someone else. If you start seeing another person, then you weaken what you have with your mate. If it weakens too much, then your mate will go find somebody else.

A husband and wife should not be too far apart. It is best for them to sleep in the same bed. When they are together a lot, this will keep the vibrations strong; they will not change. If the vibrations start to change, get closer to your partner and strengthen them again, bring them back into harmony—synchronized, matched.

The same things happens with objects, too. You love your coat, your shoes. You don't want to throw them away because they are part of your body, they are saturated with your own energy. Even though they may be worn out and look bad, you don't want to throw them away. You keep them in a corner, in a closet.

The same thing happens to a plant, to a pet, and more so to other human beings. It hurts when you break a connection. When you lose a friend, it hurts, because you break the radiations.

Now that you have completed this "mini-course" in psychometry, you know how it works, and how you can use it as a valuable part of your Everyday ESP:

o You can enter your level and charge objects in order to help people.

o You know that it can be beneficial to use tools and
   implements that have been used by good, skilled
   craftspeople.

o You know that objects can also store up negative
   emotions, such as anger and hatred, so those are best
   avoided.

o You know that living matter is also affected by the
   radiation emanating from your aura, and this includes
   the people closest to you. If you want to live in a
   peaceful, harmonious environment, then radiate peace
   and harmony. Remember: It all begins in your mind.

When you attend class with a certified Silva Method instructor,
your instructor's mind will guide your mind through a series of "mental projection" exercises so that you will then know how to project
your mind into anything—inanimate objects, plants, animals, and
humans—and detect any information that you need in order to correct a problem.

This is what we call "Effective Sensory Projection," and it is the
next step to fully developing your Everyday ESP.

Chapter 8
How to Develop ESP

ESP is a natural God-given human ability. Everybody has it, and everybody experiences it from time to time in dreams, hunches and "gut feelings," sudden insights that "come to you" unexpectedly, knowing what someone is going to say before he or she says it. Children are naturally imaginative, creative, and intuitive. But as they grow up, most of them lose their intuitive ability as they concentrate on learning the ways of the physical world and the beta-bound left brain hemisphere.

The good news is that all of us can still use our ESP when there is a need, a problem that needs to be solved. You can use the MentalVideo whenever you need it. Not for frivolous things, not for your own fun and enjoyment, but to correct problems and improve conditions on the planet for more than just yourself. If you have a serious problem to correct, you can use the MentalVideo tonight, even if you haven't yet started to learn how to enter the alpha level.

In his research, my father found that the more serious a problem is, the easier it is to use your intuition to obtain the help you need to correct it. In an emergency situation, when there is a very strong need, then very strong impressions are made on your brain neurons and all parts of your brain become active and cry out for help.

According to my father:

The more serious the nature of the problem, the more enthusiastic the person is about anything, the stronger the impression.

So we are saying that an emotional involvement is a factor. The more emotional the person is, the stronger the impression. People become emotional about problems. People become emotional about great things. So everything that's of importance, you can be assured it has been impressed very strongly because of its emotional involvement.

Minor things, things of very little value, are very faintly impressed, making it more difficult to detect this information. So the information that we use to detect it, we say, is information of value, that has been strongly impressed because of emotional involvement. This is important for problem-solving.

This is the information we need to solve problems with. Information that's necessary, that's valuable. Either because it was impressed for the survival type of response, the fight-or-flight type of response, which is strong emotional, or the enthusiastic type of discovery type of response that makes for development of problems.

There are two ways that you can learn to develop your intuition so that you can use it every day and make more correct decisions so that situations don't become serious problems. The fastest and easiest way is to learn from someone who has already established "points of reference" in the subjective dimension, became familiar with functioning in the subjective dimension, and thus developed his or her ESP and uses it daily. You can do this in just two days when you have someone there with you whose mind can guide your mind to develop those points of reference.

You can also learn on your own, but this will take more time and patience. Children between the ages of 7 and 14 pick it up easily, because they already function at the alpha range much of the time anyway. If you are older than that, you will need to learn to enter the alpha level and then use your natural ESP experiences to help you develop your own intuition.

HOW OUR SYSTEM BEGAN

It took my father three years to train my sister Isabel to be a psychic, but that wasn't what he started out to do. In the beginning, he wanted to find ways to help us remember our school lessons so we would make better grades.

But then one day, as he prepared to ask Isabel to recite some poems she had memorized, she began guessing which poem he was going to ask her to recite. When she did this several times and was correct, this aroused his curiosity and he began to investigate this "guessing faculty."

While that was unexpected, he pointed out that it was not an accident. "We didn't stumble on this by accident," he said. "We were guided every step of the way, and that's putting it lightly." Time after time, my father was the beneficiary of very fortunate "coincidences," and he felt certain that somebody or something had to be causing those coincidences to happen in order to guide him to the information he needed to learn in order to train psychics.

In the beginning he used hypnosis. But when Isabel began "guessing his mind," he realized that went beyond hypnosis. "In hypnosis you can function inductively, but not deductively," he said. "Under hypnosis you can answer questions, but you cannot ask questions, you cannot activate your mind to analyze information and solve problems. If you activate your mind, your brain comes back to the 20 cycles per second beta brain-wave frequency, unless you have learned how to keep it on 10 cycles alpha."

So, he developed a system where we could learn to lower our brain frequency on our own, and then activate our minds without returning to beta. That is what you have been learning to do in this book, and on the recording that is included with it.

Once he had taught us how to find our center, the 10 cycles alpha frequency at the center of the normal brain frequency spectrum, then he began teaching us how to develop our ESP.

He always wanted us to be able to use our ESP whenever there was a need, not just on special occasions when everything else had failed. To encourage this, he used to have us practice whenever an opportunity presented itself. When somebody would knock on our front door, he would tell us to stop and mentally detect who was there, what the person looked like. Then we could open the door and confirm it.

Of course, we only did that to develop our ability. He always cautioned us that ESP is not something we use for fun, we use it to correct problems. When we need information to help us correct a problem, then we use our ESP to detect additional information.

Eventually, after 22 years of research, he perfected a very simple and natural system for developing ESP. It works for everybody. We have millions of graduates all over the world, from every race and nationality, every religion, every age, rich people and poor, who have used our Method to develop their own natural God-given ESP.

It is easy to teach children between the ages of 7 and 14 to use their ESP, and in Chapter 14 my father will teach you how to teach your own children.

For adults, the process is different. Your mind needs to be guided by another mind, by the mind of someone who has already developed his or her ESP and uses it regularly.

How SUBJECTIVE INFORMATION IS TRANSMITTED

The mind is not a physical thing, as your body is. The mind cannot be detected with physical instruments.

Because the mind is not physical, we cannot use physical means to teach the mind what to do. We can use words and pictures to teach the body what to do, to teach your brain what to do, but when it comes to the mind, it takes another mind to teach it what to do. You can use physical means of communication to teach the body what to do, but you need mental communication to teach the mind what to do.

The mind functions in a whole different way than the body. It is sort of like dealing with computer code in that, if you look at a page of computer code, all you see are 1s and 0s. That doesn't mean anything to us human beings, but it means something to other computer code.

The computer code interacts with other computer code (instructions), and eventually it is converted into a form that you recognize:

words or pictures on your computer screen, or perhaps audio that you can hear.

For instance, you can open your word processor and depress keys on the keyboard in order to create words. The computer code that you generate when you type on the keyboard interacts with the computer code of the word processing program, which then interacts with the hardware, and eventually you can see the words on the monitor.

Mental communication is somewhat similar in that the mind subjectively (non-physically) detects subjective information about a subject, and then converts that information into a form that you can understand, such as a mental image.

The mental picture is not the actual communication. It is the end result of a mental process, just as the words on the monitor are the result of your instructions (given via the keyboard) interacting with the word-processing program, which then interacts with the computer hardware to produce light and dark pixels that you recognize as words.

If you want to detect what is inside a building in Russia (which was the first assignment given to a psychic by the CIA to determine if remote viewing was real), you go to the alpha level and project your mind to the given location.

Then your mind interacts with the subjective (non-physical) part of the object that was inside the building, detects that information, and then converts it back to a form that humans can recognize: a mental image.

The psychic, who already knew how to project his mind and detect information in this manner, was able, with his mind, to detect the subjective information about the object inside the building, and mentally convert that information into a mental picture, so that he could then tell the CIA representative what the object looked like.

A year and a half later, when the Russians rolled the object out of the building and the American U2 plane flew over and photographed it, it looked exactly the way the psychic described it 18 months earlier.

As a result of that demonstration, the CIA began a remote viewing program.

Now, how do you learn to do that?

First, you need to do it at the alpha level. At the alpha level you are able to think with both brain hemispheres.

Once you learn to enter the alpha level and then activate your mind without coming out of the 10 cycles alpha level, then you can start sharing information between the left and right brain hemispheres.

Here is the way my father explained it:

Everything that you detect with your objective (physical) senses (eyesight, hearing, smell, taste, touch) is impressed on your left brain hemisphere, and a copy is transferred to your right brain hemisphere.

Everything that you detect with your subjective (mental) senses is impressed on your right brain hemisphere. But, for most people, it is not transferred to your left brain hemisphere. That is because most of us, when we were growing up, concentrated on developing the logical left brain hemisphere, enjoying the pleasures of the physical world, and we left the right brain hemisphere behind, so to speak.

While growing up, we did not develop the use of the faculties of the right brain hemisphere: intuition, ESP.

So the first thing you need to do is to learn to function at the alpha level and to remain at alpha even after you become mentally active.

Then you can start learning how to detect the information that has been impressed on your right brain hemisphere, and transfer a copy of that information to your left brain hemisphere. We do that through the use of Mental Projection exercises.

He explained to us that when we are working with children between the ages of 7 and 14, you simply have them close their eyes and then recall things with which they are familiar, recall information that has been impressed on their left brain hemisphere.

When they do this at their level, they are synchronizing the information between the left and the right brain hemispheres.

That is what you do in a Silva seminar when you go to level and recall information about your home, when you mentally walk through your home and observe things in your home.

Then you want to go beyond that. You want to use your right brain hemisphere to detect information that you have not previously impressed with your objective (physical) senses on your left brain hemisphere.

In the Silva seminar, your instructor asks you to project yourself mentally inside a wall in your living room. You can't do that physically; you have to do it mentally. But how? There are no words we can use to explain this to your mind. Your mind needs another mind to guide it, and that's the job of your instructor's mind.

Your instructor will do the same thing that you are doing, so that your mind will have a guide. The instructor's mind will guide your mind to learn exactly what to do and how to do it. From then on, your mind will know what to do, and you can do it on your own. All you will need to do is to practice and develop your ability.

Is it possible to learn on your own, with someone else's mind to guide your mind? Of course. Approximately 10 percent of people are naturally developed psychics. So it is possible, but it might not be as easy to develop ESP on your own as some people want you to believe.

There are people who offer books, recordings, and correspondence courses, and they tell you about the people who are very successful with these courses. But ask how many of the people who take these courses are successful.

Usually it is no more than 10 percent of the total number of people who try. That's because 10 percent of people are natural alpha thinkers. Those are the ones for whom the techniques will work.

If you are one of the naturals, then you can learn to use ESP on your own fairly easily. If you are not one of the naturals, it will take you longer.

Regardless of whether you are a natural, or one of the 90 percent of us who did not learn naturally how to function at the alpha level, you can still develop your ESP in just two days when you learn Mr. Silva's Method from somebody who has already learned it, and whose mind will guide your mind through the mental exercises, so that you can establish the necessary points of reference.

A book cannot do that for you. A CD player cannot do that for you. Books and CD players don't have minds; humans do.

Once you have done the drills, then the final afternoon you will put it into practice by doing case studies. You will detect information about people with health problems. These people are not present, so you will have to detect the information at a distance.

You will do 10 of these case studies while you are still in the presence of your instructor. This is important, because you need to gain 10 experiences before you go home and start practicing on your own. Once you are on your own, you will not have your instructor's mind there to help your mind know what to do and how to function in order to detect the information.

It is a learning experience. It is like installing software and getting it configured correctly. After that, all you need to do is continue to learn how to use it, and all of the things that it is capable of doing.

You can always start with the home-study course, and if you are not making progress as quickly as you desire, then invest two days and a few hundred dollars to learn from an UltraMind ESP System instructor. Your satisfaction is guaranteed.

After you do that, all you need to do is practice and continue to establish more and more points of reference and develop your new skills.

Even if you are one of the naturals and learn quickly on your own, there are still some advantages to learning the Silva Method from an instructor. When you learn on your own, whichever way works for you is the way you will stick with. With an instructor, you get the advantage of all of the 22 years of research that my father conducted, so that you are not restricted to just one way of functioning; you establish various points of reference, which has several advantages:

- You can detect even more information because you have so many more points of reference. And you have a systematic approach that you can return to in order to continue to be just as successful every time, and more so every time you practice.

- In order to learn on your own, do what my father had us do as children: "Guess" at things, and when you are correct, enter your level and review the experience, especially the feeling that you had when you were correct. As you accumulate more and more of these "points of reference," you will find that your accuracy increases, and you will use your Everyday ESP more and more frequently.

Section III:
Better Health

Chapter 9
Overcoming Health Problems

The first area where we need to apply our Everyday ESP is health because good health is so important. My father put it this way:

If you are not healthy, you are not going to do anything else, you will not be able to fulfill your mission. You can obtain guidance to help you make the right decisions to regain good health if you need to do that, as well as guidance and support about nutrition, exercise, stress management, and other things to ensure you have ample energy to achieve what you need to achieve.

He discovered long ago that there are many things you can do to improve and maintain good health, and plenty of energy to do your job. In just a moment we will discuss how you can use your mind to help correct health problems, both for yourself and for others, and also how you can qualify for and obtain help from higher intelligence when you encounter a problem that you cannot solve on your own. But first, a brief explanation about how and why this works.

In the 1950s, my father began to research the field of holistic faith healing and learn how it worked. He became quite a good healer himself, and, even better, he developed holistic faith healing techniques that anybody can learn to use to correct health problems for themselves and others.

He used everything from hypnosis and suggestion to laying-on-of-hands to prayer healing at great distances, and over the last four decades we have shown millions more people how to do the same. Using scientific methodology, he developed the "repeatable experiment," and demonstrated time and again that it works. Plenty of Silva graduates will attest to that.

But scientists always want to know *why* it works. For the last 20 years, a scientist named Bruce Lipton, a cell biologist, has approached this from the biological point of view, and his research has not only met up with my father's research, it overlaps and confirms it.

Similar to many scientists, Dr. Lipton said he didn't allow much room for religious or spiritual philosophies in his research. He wanted objective, physical, explanations. But he ran into a problem that he was having difficulty solving. He explained:

> The whole thing we are teaching about DNA is wrong. What I was teaching students in medical schools didn't really conform to the way life was controlled. The whole idea that DNA is a self-actualizing molecule is wrong. Leading edge science is providing people with an understanding of how our beliefs and perceptions control the gene. Whatever it is that controls our physical body is not from within our physical body, it plays through it via mechanisms on the cell surface.
>
> When I started to realize that my thoughts affect my cells, I began to think that the thoughts and feelings that I have are like a government to a community of about 50 trillion cells. Our mind represents the collective consciousness of 50 trillion cells. Every cell has a digestive system, a respiratory system, an immune system, every system that we have as human beings.
>
> (Coast to Coast AM with George Noory, February 9, 2005)

Our thoughts broadcast to our cells, he said. Individual cells observe everything we observe. Based on the reports from the mind, they are either in a state of growth, or in a state of protection, where they are not allowed to grow, not allowed to do the jobs they are supposed to do. If we are broadcasting fear to our cells, they will go into protection mode. In the absence of growth, cells will get sick and can die.

Dr. Lipton noted that scientists have been saying that DNA is the "brain of the cell" and controls our cells, which in turn control the body and its functions. However, when you take the genes out of the cell, it still functions the same as before. The nucleus is not the brain of the cell, it is the gonads, it is reproduction. It rebuilds the cell and replaces worn-out parts.

So where is the brain of the cell, he wondered. He explains how to answer came to him in a flash of insight one night:

> That's what I was working on one night in 1985, at 1:59 in the morning. Suddenly I understood, and in an instant my life changed completely. I went from a nonspiritual person to a spiritually understanding person because I saw how the mechanism worked.
>
> I was writing a biochemical definition of the cell membrane, and I wrote that "the cell membrane is a liquid crystal semi-conductor with gates and channels." I looked at that, and thought, *I read that definition somewhere.* But I had no idea where. It wasn't in biology. I looked up and there was my first Macintosh computer, and a book from Radio Shack, a simpleton book about understanding your microprocessor, and on page 3 of the introduction it said that "a chip is a crystal semi-conductor with gates and channels." For a millisecond or two there was a storm of activity in my head. I thought, it was so coincidental, but it wasn't a coincidence.
>
> It has now been demonstrated that the cell membrane is an organic information processing chip. It picks up information from the environment, because the surface of a cell is the molecular equivalent of a keyboard, made out of receptor proteins. It detects information, just like your eyes and ears and taste buds do. The cell has the molecular equivalent of these. Signals going to the receptors on the surface of the cell send a message *into* the cell which can control the genes so that the cell makes an appropriate response to stay alive in the environment. (Noory, 1995)

All Macintosh computers had the same kind of processor, yet this processor could do a wide variety of things: It could write letters, it could draw pictures, it could do math, it could even run a business if you gave it the right instructions. When you understand the nature of the programming, you don't go in and change the machine when you have a problem, you have to understand how to reprogram the machine.

That is the key: the instructions. Different instructions will cause it to do different things. The same processor could perform many different tasks depending on the instructions that were sent to it.

The next question then is: Where do the instructions come from?

The obvious answer is that the instructions come from the brain. The brain sends instructions, and the DNA carries out those instructions.

But then that brings up another question: Where does the brain get the instructions from?

The mind. The mind guides the brain, and the brain guides the body.

It was another moment of enlightenment for Dr. Lipton, as he realized the power that our thoughts can have over our health. This is the same thing that my father had found in his research and experimentation. In addition to affecting our own body, our thoughts and words can also influence other people's brains and bodies.

We communicate with one another all the time, through our words, our actions, our auras, and our thoughts. We have all had the experience of someone lifting our spirits, or bringing them down, just by his or her presence. My father found that the physical part of the aura extends about 8 meters from the body, so if we are within 8 meters (25 feet) of one another, we are exchanging physical energy.

The influence of the mind, of course, is not limited by distance. Quantum physicists have demonstrated a phenomenon they call "entanglement" that can exist from one side of the universe to the other. Particles on opposite sides of the universe react to each other simultaneously. That's because they exist simultaneously in a nonphysical dimension, which we call the subjective dimension, where there is no time and space. That is the dimension where the mind functions.

Of course another question eventually occurred to Dr. Lipton: Where does the mind get the ideas from? From some kind of higher power?

"I have never considered myself a particularly religious person," Dr. Lipton said. "But the scientific conclusions that I have come to sound a lot like what religions have been saying."

His thinking has now expanded far beyond the genes and cells of the body. He now thinks of planet earth as an organism and the humans who populate it as cells within that organism.

Each person is composed of a set of cells that are unique to that individual human being. Signals are coming from the environment, and each of us uses the signals that are unique to us.

You could compare it to white light coming through a prism. The prism breaks the light up into the rainbow spectrum comprised of millions of colors, and each of us represents a particular wavelength of the spectrum that we need. So we are each individuals, but collectively, we are white light. (Noory, 1995)

We can and must learn to function properly, he said.

This has now become his mission. Health is still the first order of business because it is so important to our individual survival. We must have vibrant good health in order to have the energy to do the work we were sent here to do. And that mission, Dr. Lipton has concluded, is to pay attention to the signals that are being sent to us—to the messages from higher intelligence—and begin to function together in harmony for the common good.

If not, humanity will wind up like a diseased organ, with cells malfunctioning and not contributing to the well-being of the organism. That creates a condition known as dis-ease, which causes suffering, which limits our ability to function as we should, and can eventually lead to cessation of existence—death. According to Dr. Lipton:

> We have to stop killing one another. We are all part of the same living organism called humanity. To eliminate another person is the same as going into your body and ripping out cells and throwing them away.
>
> Just as single celled creatures evolved into more complex forms, humanity will eventually merge into a larger organization or being. This in turn will lead to complete harmony with the Earth, which could then take its place as an intergalactic being. (Noory, 1995)

My father came to the same conclusions from a mental and spiritual point of view. During his research in the 1960s he was trying hard to understand what he was experiencing. "How could a common man like me heal a priest?" he asked. "Compared to a man who has been a priest for 20 years, I am just a sinner. How can a sinner heal a priest?"

Then one Sunday, while attending services at Christ the King Church, just up the street from our house, he heard the answer in the sermon. The priest told the story about the Roman Centurion who had a servant who was ill, and had been unable to cure him. So the Centurion sought out the Jewish healer named Jesus and asked him to help.

According to the story, Jesus first made sure that the Centurion really believed that he could help, then told the Centurion to take him to the servant and he would work on him.

The Centurion said that it wasn't necessary for Christ to go in person. The Centurion knew his servant, and it was his responsibility to take care of his servant, but this time he needed some help from somebody with more power than he had. He simply wanted Christ to use him, the Centurion, as the vehicle to send the help to the servant.

We are in the position of the Centurion. We have been entrusted with the responsibility to take care of planet earth. We have been given the tools and the authority to do it. We can use our mind to heal the body—our own body, as well as other people's bodies—by sending the correct instructions to the genes.

But sometimes we run into problems for which we don't have the solution. Then, like the Centurion, we need to go to a higher authority for guidance and help. "It is not our place to put God to work," my father told us. "We were sent here to do the work. But when we are doing all that we can do and we still need more help, we can certainly ask, and we will receive the help, if our efforts are of a constructive and creative nature," he said.

You can learn more about Dr. Lipton's work from his book *The Biology of Belief: Unleashing the Power of Consciousness, Matter and Miracles* (Mountain of Love/Elite Books 2005), which is available from major booksellers, and also available from his Website (*www.brucelipton.com*), along with a freely downloadable articles about the "new" science and other sound and video recordings.

Right now, let's take a look at what you can do to help your health and the health of your loved ones, and review some case studies of people who are actually applying these techniques.

When you have a health problem, you can use the 3-Scenes Technique that we covered in Chapter 5 to correct it. This is how you can send instructions to your genes. Just send mental images of the problem and the solution.

When someone else has a problem, you can enter your level while in their presence—within the aura range—and program to help correct his or her health problem. Use the 3-Scenes Technique in exactly the same way in order to send instructions to his or her genes.

My father said that there is a mold provided by higher intelligence, a blueprint of the perfect body. He called it the "Soul Mold." He said that "The soul is a mold that holds matter together. It is adhesive and cohesive." We cannot alter this mold—only God can do that—but we can reinforce it. By sending mental images, you can attract matter to return to the confines of the mold, the perfect blueprint created by the Creator.

Dr. Lipton says, "the cell membrane is an organic information chip that reacts to the environment." It reacts to the messages sent to it—our thoughts, our words, and our programming.

"We are not automatons to our genes," he explains. "We all contain a metropolis of 50 trillion citizens, the cells in our body, which could each be considered sentient beings in their own right, yet they act together as a community. You have 50 trillion cells living together in perfect harmony under your skin. Humanity needs to learn to do the same."

Dr. Lipton says that the energy that creates this "community of cells" acts like a "magnetic field," causing the cells to assemble into a certain pattern.

"Imagine if I take a piece of paper and sprinkle iron filings on it," he explained. "Every time you do that, you just get a random pile of iron filings. But if I put a magnet underneath that piece of paper, then every time I sprinkle iron filings they form the shape of the magnet's invisible field. If I make a complex pattern of magnets, I get a complex pattern of iron filings. If I throw away the iron filings and sprinkle new ones, guess what: it forms the same pattern again.

"The iron filings are like cells, and there is a field with information. Without that energy field, you just have a pile of random cells and it doesn't form anything."

My father called that energy field the "Soul Mold." He explained, "The soul is a mold that holds matter together. It is cohesive and adhesive. The mold comes from higher intelligence, from the Creator." We humans have been made in the image of our Creator, not in how we look physically, but in what we can do. "Image is of the mind," he said. "We can use the mind to help correct problems with the creation."

When you hold an image of perfect health in your mind, and do this in relation to a specific person, you are strengthening the energy field that holds matter together into the complex pattern that makes up an organ, for instance. By strengthening the energy field, you are helping to attract cells back to the mold, to the perfect pattern of a healthy organ.

That's what happens when you use the 3-Scenes Technique. First you identify the problem, and the person who has the problem. Then you incorporate into your programming whatever is being done to help correct the problem, and imagine this attracting the cells back to the perfect pattern. And you finish with an image of a perfect organ, a perfectly healthy human being whose body conforms to the perfect energy pattern that the Creator provided.

Higher intelligence is also sending signals to us about how to behave, how to interact with one another, what we must do in order to remain healthy as individuals, as a family, as a community, and as a group known as humanity on planet earth. You can use the MentalVideo to obtain this information. If we follow the instructions and conform to the plan provided by higher intelligence, we will be healthy and prosperous.

In the next chapter we'll look at some examples to see exactly how we can put this into action.

Chapter 10

Examples of ESP for Fitness and Health

Higher intelligence often knows better than we do. Sometimes we are guided to use physical medicine to help us even if we are reluctant to do so, and other times the guidance steers us away from what we, with our limited intelligence, think is best. Here are two examples.

FINDING THE RIGHT DOCTOR

Have you ever worried about whether you were making the correct decision about how to deal with a health problem? Can you take care of it holistically? Should you resort to drugs? Do you need surgery in order to correct it?

The wrong decision could be costly, both in money and also in its affect on your life. It could leave you in pain and unable to fulfill your responsibilities on your job, and in your family.

After you have gathered all of the objective data you can find, your next step in using your Everyday ESP to help you correct the problem is the 3-Scenes Technique. Visualize the problem, then visualize yourself obtaining information and making good decisions and getting better as you take steps to get well, and then imagine yourself in perfect health once again. As you mentally picture yourself in perfect health in the third scene, recall the feeling of being in excellent health, recall the things you do, the way you think, the way you talk.

That's a good start, but does it remove the lingering doubt that you are doing the best thing? After you talk to doctors and friends, after you search the Internet and scour your local library and gather all of the information you can find, after you go to your level and analyze all of that information at the alpha level, and after you use your mind to scan your own body and detect exactly what's going on (as you learn to do in the live seminars), wouldn't it be great if there were still one more source with even more information, as well as an excellent track record at making the right decisions?

There is such a source. After you have looked at all of the information you can find, and listened to all of the suggestions that everybody has, there is another source, which my father called "your invisible means of support."

You can use the MentalVideo to obtain guidance from your tutor, in the spiritual dimension, on the "other side" as some people call it. Your tutor is your personal connection to the hierarchy of God.

This is not a substitute for making your own investigation. The more information you can provide to your tutor when you do your MentalVideo, the better results and guidance you will receive. That's what happened to Catherine Ong of Australia when she was unsure that she was getting the best advice and making the best decision. Here is what Catherine wrote to us in June of 2002.

Hi there Ed,

First of all, thank you very much for programming for me. I wrote you back on May 12th about my scheduled surgery to remove a patch of calcifications (possibly indicating cancer) in my right breast.

Well, some interesting things happened after that. The night before, I decided that instead of feeling frightened, I should go to level and "talk" to the calcifications. I felt that maybe understanding why they were there and what (specifically) had caused them to develop, might help me encourage them to leave and allow me to stay free of them and other illnesses in the future.

I then moved on to alpha-healing visualizations and a final prayer broadcasting for helpful people to come into my life to help me with this.

I awoke in the middle of the night, convinced my mother (who died in 1977) had warned me not to go ahead with the surgery. Normally, I am not someone to question authority, but I was determined to follow the advice of my Mum (who I know represents my own deep levels of mind). Instead of simply making a phone call, I went to the hospital to cancel the surgery in person and ended up waiting for hours. I went outside for a change of scene, and "happened to" see the doctor who had delivered my second son six years ago. I took this "coincidence" as a sign that it was help from the other side, and approached her. Although she probably did not remember me from before, this harried, tired woman took me under her wing and put me in touch with a specialist breast surgeon, arranging a meeting that very evening. He usually has a waiting list of months!

I am so, so glad I followed my intuition and I am so so glad that I had the tools developed by Jose Silva to help me help myself. Almost everything that has happened to me since that night of coming "face to face" with my problem at level has been charmed. I only have Silva to thank for that.

This new doctor has been an angel for me and my husband. He has spent many hours educating us, and involving us in every decision made. He explains everything thoroughly and has helped me deal with all that has come up, physically and emotionally. He has helped me—and, just as importantly, my whole family—through this process. He is a doctor with his heart as well as his profession.

As it turned out, I did have cancer—one called ductal carcinoma in situ. I will find out soon if it was confined to the ducts (best news possible). I did need to have surgery, but it was not as radical as the first doctor had proposed. I have been home from hospital since Saturday and am still medicated quite heavily and a not much practical use to anyone yet ;-p, but I plan on being better and better every day, and ultimately even better than before.

I will probably need to have a course of radiation therapy, as the cancer was rated high-grade, which means it has advanced enough to cause concern that it may have tipped over into becoming invasive. I feel confident that it has not, but please continue to keep me in mind, won't you?

Catherine Ong, Australia

June 2002

Not only did Catherine get over the cancer, but a couple of years later she even signed up to become a Silva UltraMind ESP Systems instructor.

ESP IN MEDICAL PRACTICE

Perhaps the best doctor is one who uses Everyday ESP in his practice, and one such doctor is Calvin Poole M.D., of Gloster, Mississippi. He knows both sides of the story. He was in a coma after a terrible accident, and used the alpha level and the Silva techniques to get rid of the headaches and recover so completely that he was able to resume his medical practice.

Here are some experiences he sent us recently.

While working the ER, I was seeing a lot of patients with stomach viruses. It is not always the excitement that one sees on television. With so many people coming in, it is impossible and unnecessary to do a full work-up on everyone.

I picked up one of the charts and a voice said, "This one has an appendicitis." I told the nurses and they said, "But you haven't even seen the patient yet." I went ahead and started a work-up on him. Everything was equivocal, so I did a CT (computerized tomography) with IV (intravenous) and oral contrast. This showed up an appendicitis!

What was weird is that another patient came in several days later, and it was a replay of the same thing. Pick up the chart, make the diagnosis, get the studies ordered, see the patient—not the usual pattern for diagnosis. The surgeon called me later and told me that he had an early appendicitis, but not bad.

I have had some emergencies come in, and wondered, "How in the world am I going to manage this?" I got out of the way and let something else take over, and got good results on all of them.

I had one episode of a woman stepping on a nail, and it breaking off in her foot. Removing it is one of the most difficult things to do with all the tendons and connective tissue. It was a very small nail, like an upholstery nail, not much bigger than a straight pin.

Suddenly, the idea of using fluoroscopy came up. I think someone said it, but who knows?

I went back and worked on it for about 45 minutes. I could get close, but could not get it. I said, "I give up," clicked the hemostats closed, which I normally would not have done, pulled them out, and it had the nail that I had been looking for.

Thanks again on behalf of both me and my patients, most of whom would not have believed that method that I was trained in and used.

Dr. Poole has also been trained to teach the Silva UltraMind ESP System. There is information about how to contact him and other Silva instructors in the appendix.

LIBBY AND KARL

A lady in Canada named Libby ordered a copy of the UltraMind ESP System home-study course from Avlis Productions, and what ensued shows the power of coincidence when you are using the techniques that my father developed. Ed Bernd Jr. and Katherine Handorf handled it, so I will let them tell you what happened.

We notified Libby that we wanted to insure the package and therefore could not send it to a post office box. Why the Canadian postal authorities won't accept an insured package that is mailed to their post office is a mystery to us!

Libby told us that her husband, Karl, was sick and she was ordering the home study course so she could learn how to program to help him. So we used the MentalVideo Technique that night with the idea of getting all the help for Libby and Karl that we could.

When we heard back from Libby the next day, she told us that Karl had an 5.3 cm aortic aneurysm located just below the breast bone, and it was leaking and could burst at any moment and kill him. They were waiting for a hospital room so he could go for surgery. He only had one kidney and all of the stress was impairing its functioning too. So she wanted to know if there was a faster way to get the program to her.

We told her that we'd send it via Federal Express so it would be there within two days, and that we would also send the information about Karl to some Silva graduates who like to work health cases and help those who need it.

It was about 2 a.m. when we sent the e-mail to the graduates and we made a little "mistake." While adding a lot of names to the blind carbon copy line in the address section, Ed "accidentally" included a woman named Dolores, who is not an UltraMind graduate. She completed the UltraMind home study course but had not learned yet how to do distant healing, which is taught in the live class. Ed was thinking of a different woman. A few minutes after he sent the e-mail, he realized his "mistake," and sent a copy to the woman he had originally intended, who had recently graduated from the course and was looking for health cases to work.

Ed was concerned about getting the people mixed up, but the next day we got a note from Dolores thanking us for including her, and promising to program for Karl and Libby. Dolores had had a lot of success in a difficult job situation using the MentalVideo. Recently, she was told she was being laid off, and despite a tight job market, received two job offers and found another job in a very short time. After that we suggested to her that she program for some of her coworkers who also needed new jobs, and she did.

The next day we heard from Libby. Karl had gotten a hospital room. Doctors rushed to examine him when they saw the medical reports about how serious his condition was. They were a bit confused. The aneurysm had shrunk from 5.3 cm to 2.1 cm and it wasn't leaking. His one kidney, which had shut down, began working again. Libby said he was now "peeing like a puppy." In fact, she said it three times in her e-mail.

In addition, Karl had been suffering from excruciating hip pain and the pain was completely gone, it mysteriously disappeared even though nothing was done medically for it. She said she was thankful for the problems with mailing to a Canadian post office box because if not for that, she probably would never have told us about Karl's condition and gotten so many outstanding healers working on him.

We passed the word on to everybody who had helped. A few days later we heard from Dolores again. Working on Karl had given her the idea that maybe she could work on her 80-year-old mother. She did, and when she talked with her mother a couple days later, her mother was really excited and upbeat, and showed improvement from pain that had been limiting her mobility for the past few years. She was even talking about taking a trip to visit relatives in another state, something she had not felt up to doing for a long time because of her pain. There had been no changes made to her mother's medications, and her doctors had previously told her there wasn't much they could do for her. They told her she would just have to learn to deal with the pain.

Ed wrote to Dolores and praised her, and congratulated her on her success with her mother, and then he admitted his "mistake" in sending her the e-mail about Karl and Libby.

Dolores wrote back saying that she was laughing, and asked if he really thought it was a mistake, because so many good things resulted from that event. (Of course not, that's why he put "mistake" in quotes.) She said that right after she programmed for her coworkers, she began to wonder what else she could do to help people. She said that three days before Ed "mistakenly" sent her Karl's case, she had programmed with a MentalVideo that she would be provided with ideas on how she could best apply the Silva System to help people, and to get practice to improve her skills. She sent a report to her "tutor"—her personal representative on the "other side." She then acted on the mental video guidance she received (the case we sent her by "mistake"), by choosing to use the 3-Scenes Technique to program for help for Karl, and then later for her mother.

Here is how we think it works: Her tutor passed the word to other tutors, and when Ed's tutor heard about it, checked to see what he was up to. So at 2 a.m., trying to remember the people who like to work cases, he got a little "confused" and typed the name *Dolores* instead of *Kathryn.* Then a few minutes later he realized his "mistake" and sent a copy of the e-mail to Kathryn. Why do I think the tutor did all of that? Because Ed had used the MentalVideo the night before.

There's one more note to the story of Libby and Karl: Turns out that Karl has two aneurisms—a small one and a large one. At the hospital, they only saw the small one. Evidently that "mistake" bought them enough time so that they ended up making the correct decision. There are some other unanticipated benefits too.

Libby sent us an e-mail and explained it this way:

Karl's home doctor, Dr. Smith, phoned this morning to tell him that because two doctors were working on him he was discharged before things were explained to him properly.

Apparently the measurement of 5.3 cm isn't as "dire" as they thought, and since the surgery of this type to repair the aneurysm is more critical than the aneurysm itself at this time, surgery has been postponed and he has to go back for CT scans every three months so they can keep an eye on it.

We were all delighted when we got the news that it had shrunk to only 2.1 cm, especially when there was no medical explanation. It turns out he has two aneurysms, the smaller and the larger.

We all know that things happen for a reason and I believe the reason is to give Karl and the healers working on him a little more time. Please keep your group working on him to "heal and repair" both aneurysms and to get his pinched nerve unpinched.

Karl is working with me on the home study course to learn centering. I believe that Karl's "Mission" is to become a healer. The few times he has meditated, he immediately pictures colors, and is able to do distant viewing quite easily. Can you imagine how hard his tutor is trying to get his attention! They sure must be frustrated with him.

He got a big scare when the doc phoned this morning and has been asking a lot of "Psychic/Spiritual" questions. He's now ready and his teachers have indeed appeared. <chuckle>

Thanks once again for all the help coming from The Gang at Silva.

Libby:-)

A COMMON RECURRING PROBLEM

Sometimes people don't think to use the Silva Method until they have a big life-threatening problem such as the ones discussed in the previous section. You don't have to wait for a major problem, you can use your Everyday ESP for common problems that affect many people, such as the problem that one woman, working as an assistant for Mme Xue Kuiyang, the first UltraMind trainer in China, had. Here is her story:

During every menstruation period, I had abdominal pain. So that was what I depicted in the first MentalVideo, the problem video.

Then in the solution video, I pictured myself smiling with no pain at all.

Then I sent them out at alpha and went to sleep.

The next morning, I did not have any signs that indicated a solution to the problem.

After the day's work, I followed Mme Xue Kuiyang to the Saite Hotel to visit one of her British friends. Xue purchased some gifts for her friend, including two boxes of Lipton Red Tea. Then we went to dinner. When I came back home, I found that my menstruation had come, but I didn't feel any pain.

Early the next morning, I felt pain. Suddenly, I saw the Lipton Red Tea. Then I remembered that I had heard from a friend that red tea is more useful and effective as a pain killer than medication is. So I drank one cup of red tea and felt relieved of the pain.

Later on I told Mme Xue about this experience. She told me that it was guidance from higher intelligence. She bought the tea because when she saw the Lipton Red Tea, she remembered that her husband loved it. But she gave me one box as well so that I could try it out.

PREVENTIVE MEDICINE

It is wonderful to have the ability to correct problems. It is even better to have the ability to prevent them, to head them off before they can cause you any trouble.

Here is the story of one young man's experience, exactly as he wrote it to us:

Earlier this year I purchased the Silva UltraMind home study course and thought it was great and started studying it straight away.

My situation at the time was that I was on long-term sick leave from my job. I was bankrupt and going through a divorce, and to make matters worse, I had a bust-up with my father and was booted out of the house.

For some reason I had the idea to try to start a new life in Thailand: to find work and maybe set up a business. My friends said I was crazy and just about everyone tried to talk me out of it. But I just had the feeling that something was telling me to go there.

The very day I started to travel to Thailand, all kinds of things were going wrong, and after a few weeks disaster struck when I had everything stolen from me.

This left me in a completely desperate situation. With no money, passport, or flight ticket, I was completely stuck in Thailand, where I could eventually face detention by the authorities and then be deported. In addition, the people who I thought were my friends turned their back on me and would not help.

I was in a completely negative frame of mind, feeling insecure about my future, feeling very angry and bitter about life. But then I realized all this time I had completely forgotten about using the Silva methods. So I started to do the Long Relaxation Exercise just to calm me down, and things started to change.

My father sent me some money (which was a miracle), my wife sent me some money (another miracle), and an associate over here even made arrangements to get me a new passport.

So my situation has improved, although I am still here at the moment as I never seem to have enough money to completely leave the country. I am still working on ideas to make a business and earn money, as there is still potential.

David Marvesley

Here is an example of how helping someone else can bring you benefits, too:

I have been listening to those CDs and I'm beginning to have some successes here and there.

For instance, flying back from Atlanta yesterday, I sat beside this young girl who was having a real bad time. Before we took off, she coughed a lot and could hardly keep her tissues off her nose. Nobody had to tell me she was miserable.

I went to level and asked for help for her; I pictured her feeling better, the cough letting up, and her having a nicer flight in general.

Shortly after take off, she became quiet and soon dozed off. Not a cough until we landed at Dulles. I gave thanks to higher intelligence.

Julie Obi

January 2004

Another type of "preventive medicine" is making the correct decisions to keep your body healthy and vibrant.

We all need to exercise the body to keep it healthy. Exercise will give you the strength, endurance, and vitality that you need to do your job and fulfill your life's mission.

But what kind of exercise is best for you? You can ask yourself that question, level, and perhaps come up with the right answer. You can also seek guidance from higher intelligence.

One Silva graduate read about the benefits of jogging and decided that was right for him. However, he didn't get the kind of benefits he had read about. First of all, it was hard for him to jog even one mile. And to make matters worse, he developed shin splints.

So he sought guidance, and the next day he noticed someone riding a bicycle. She seemed to be enjoying herself, and the graduate recalled how much he enjoyed riding a bicycle when he was young. So he checked the want ads for garage sales, and bought himself an inexpensive bicycle.

It worked out great. He found that he could ride for an hour at a time without any problems. "It was great to be able to get my exercise while sitting down," he said with a grin. It didn't hurt his shins, or any other part of his body. And he got measurable results: "In just a few weeks," he reported, "my resting pulse rate had dropped 10 points, from 72 beats per minute to 62."

You can also use the MentalVideo for guidance about what kind of food is best for you to eat. Bill Sturdevant, our UltraMind instructor in Juneau, Alaska, got an unexpected surprise one day after using the MentalVideo the night before to obtain some guidance.

Bill asked his sister Molly to pick up some cilantro for him when she went to the grocery store. She came back with a bag of green stuff, but it wasn't cilantro. She had picked up parsley "by mistake." Of course we know that there are no "mistakes" when we are programming correctly. So he got out a book about the nutritional and healing properties of foods and looked up parsley. Sure enough, it had exactly the properties for which he was looking.

It might take you a little while to get used to the way the MentalVideo works. The natural inclination might be to get annoyed that she brought back the "wrong" thing. Once you get used to using the MentalVideo, then you will be on the lookout for "indications" that can guide you in the correct direction.

SAFETY

Safety is certainly important. Better to invest a little time staying safe rather than having to invest time and effort to heal an injury. Here are a couple examples.

This e-mail is from Mme Xue Kuiyang, the first certified UltraMind ESP System instructor in China.

> On February 16, 2005, I finished my instructor training and was on my way back home. I just had transferred in Amsterdam and got on the airplane.
>
> I was sitting in my seat and waiting for the plane to take off. Suddenly I became quite uneasy. So I naturally went into level and asked for the reason.
>
> On my mental screen, there appeared a rectangular iron box, which contained fluids inside and was supposed to be full. But it was leaking fast, nearly a third of it was gone. I came out of the level and asked one of the flight attendants to check if there was something like the box in the airplane.
>
> She said that everything was fine with the airplane. But I saw her calling somebody, and then she walked away.
>
> Fifteen minutes later, while she was walking toward me, the uneasiness disappeared. She came to me and asked, "Are you a clairvoyant?"

I told her that I just had half a year of ESP training. She said, "Thank you very much."

This report is from our friend Dolores, who lives in the Northeastern United States. She started with the home study course and then attended the UltraMind ESP System seminar.

A month ago, almost to the day, I was driving a 200 mile trip west across the state to visit friends. I had RSVPed that I would attend a special event that they spent weeks preparing for. I didn't realize, until I got 100 miles into my trip and stopped in a tiny little town that I always stop in for lunch when I travel, that everything was closed down. There was no power.

Not even the one grocery store in town was open, not even the gas station. No cell phone signals available to find out what was going on or to call my friends to find out what was going on over where they were. I was "in the middle of nowhere." I took a bite of a granola bar from a box I threw in the car at the last moment that morning and a couple swigs of water.

Then I managed to tune into an emergency travel radio station with a weak staticky signal. I understood enough to hear that there was a huge power outage across the state, no gas stations open for at least the next 100 miles.

Next nearest town was 50 miles away over a snowy mountain pass, and I knew there would have no power when I reached it. I looked at my gauge and saw that I still had 3/4 of a tank of gas. Not certain what to do at this point, I went to level and asked for an assessment of the situation: Should I continue on to my friends who I had promised I'd be there?

Based on the answer I received, I decided to continue on my trip rather than turn around and head back home again.

When I drove through Seattle, it was eerie and calm as could be, a temperature inversion had settled in, 30 degrees, no power for people's heat and lights, to operate thousands of gasoline pumps, traffic signals, and support services. More than a million residences were affected and out of luck, and that doesn't include all the businesses and surrounding towns.

There were long lines of unsuspecting travelers lined up at the few gas stations equipped with emergency power to operate pumps. More than a million people were without power for what went on for over a week in many areas, not to mention all the property damage.

I found out that the power outage was caused by a storm of extremely high winds the night before, knocking down thousands of trees that knocked down power lines, damaged property, injured people. We had the same high winds over here on the east side, but we weren't affected. Our desert climate doesn't support many trees. I didn't suspect a thing, no mention on the news about a power outage when I set out that morning on my trip.

Also, if you can imagine thousands of people all burning wood in their wood stoves at the same time for days to keep warm during a temperature inversion, the lucky ones with woodstoves, that is, the stench of the smoke and what it does to your lungs and eyes. It was like driving through a forest fire.

As it turned out, my friends live in one of the few towns on the west side of the state that was unaffected by the massive power outage, and I made it to my destination without a single delay. I already knew I would make it there, that everything would be fine when I got there. I "saw" it when I was at level.

HELP OTHERS

Larisa Nikiforova attended the UltraMind seminar at New York in March 2005, and had immediate success with the MentalVideo. Here is what she wrote:

On the first day of the workshop we learned how to use the MentalVideo Technique. It has three parts. We did two parts in class and needed to do the third part before we went to sleep.

I worked on my physical problem. I couldn't sit cross-legged. The problem started a month ago and it was getting worse. I am a healer and I talk to my body all the time. I was getting messages of what I could do to help myself, but I also felt that I was not getting a complete answer. I decided to give the MentalVideo Technique a try, because it is supposed to work when we need guidance.

I did the technique on Saturday night and forgot about it. On Wednesday I had an ear candling client and decided to use the 3-Scenes Technique, which we learned on Sunday, 30 minutes before the session.

I visualized the client and how I was helping her with her problem, and I asked the Universe that if the woman liked the session, I would like her to recommend me to someone else if it was for her, mine, and the other person's higher good. I am very careful of how I use my power.

When I saw my client, she moved and looked exactly the way I imagined her to. She left after the session, and my friend, who works at the metaphysical store where I do healing work, asked me if I had time to stay a little bit longer and have some tea with her. I had one hour and a half till the next client. I went to the next room to get a cup and the man came in. I had seen him once, but didn't remember much about him. My friend and I invited him to have tea with us and he said that he had more then an hour till his next client and would love to have some tea and chat. He has an office nearby.

We started talking and I confessed to him that I didn't remember his name and what he does. He told me that he is a massage therapist and also practices a Rosen method. The ring of the store's phone interrupted our conversation. My client, who had just left, was calling and asking if I could do an ear candling session for her husband. We scheduled an appointment, and when I put the phone down, I knew that the 3-Scenes Technique was working very fast. I was very surprised.

Then the man and I continued our conversation, and I asked his opinion about my physical problem and he offered me a session. The switch turned on in my head and I knew that the offer was the result of using the MentalVideo Technique.

I had the session right away in the next room on my healing table. I visualized the number 3 in my inner eye at the beginning of the session and knew that I would have at least three sessions. My body became lighter and more flexible after just one session. It was amazing. I am buying a gift certificate for my friend and two more sessions for me.

In conclusion, I would like to say that I am very glad that I attended the Silva UltraMind seminar. I have read many self-help books, attended many workshops, practiced different techniques, but still was looking for something else and I found it at this seminar. These techniques are so simple that I wonder why I didn't invent them myself.

Larisa Nikiforova

Mount Kisco, NY

Psychometry comes in handy in preventing problems, as well as correcting them. Here is what Joanne Larkins did after receiving the UltraMind home-study course:

After listening to the Silva UltraMind ESP home-study course over Christmas, I decided to program presents, angel pins, with health, riches, wisdom, happiness, love, and luck. If nothing else, everyone that received a pin had a glowing smile.

In programming the angel pins, I held the angel pins, which were in a plastic bag, to my chest as I went to level. When I was at level, I said to myself that I wanted the pins to have health, richness, happiness, luck, and love, so that whoever would wear the pin, whatever that person most needed in his or her life that is the area that the pin would concentrate on for that person, so the circumstances that would solve his or her need would happen.

Perhaps I did not do it correctly, but since my intention was based on the five Laws of Programming, in which doing the greater good was up-permost in my mind, and I truly wanted the people who received the pin to feel better about themselves, and that good things would happen to them, I can only hope that I did some good, and that it was done correctly.

Joanne Larkins

HELP AND BE HELPED

Before we leave this topic, I want to pass on a word of advice from Temple Nash, a Silva UltraMind ESP Systems instructor in Dallas, Texas: *Remember that you are a messenger, you are not the source of the healing.*

"Yogananda said in his book that there was a yogi who used his energy to heal others," Temple said, "and having used it all up, he died. Preferring to not have that result, I have been a conduit for many years. The cosmos provides me with a limitless supply so I need not be concerned about using it all up. Good thing, too, because it flows through me like a river."

I hope that these stories of ordinary people just like you and me will encourage you to use your Everyday ESP and be a conduit to send the healing energy to anyone and everyone you happen to hear of who needs it. It only takes a moment, and it could change a person's life for the better.

And remember, when the healing energy is flowing through you to someone else, some of it sticks to you, so you also benefit from it. Isn't that a wonderful system?

Thank you.

Chapter 11
Programmed Dreams
by Prof. Clancy D. McKenzie, M.D.

Programmed dreams offer a breakthrough in medical and psychiatric diagnosis and treatment. I first learned the technique from the Silva training in September 1969, and I have been using it ever since.

You may have heard about problems being solved or discoveries being made during sleep or during the dream-state. These are mostly sporadic events, in which people just happen to awaken with a bright idea.

The programmed dream is different. It gives us the ability to awaken with that bright idea or solution to a problem, any night, at will.

You do not have to be a yogi and meditate for 50 years in a cave to achieve enlightenment. You reach just as deep a level of consciousness when you fall asleep—but you are unaware of this state and how to use it.

Utilizing the Silva techniques, you will be able to spend one minute prior to going to bed to formulate a question, and one minute when you awaken to retrieve the answer.

There are two techniques I use, and more are taught in the Silva training program. The first is to decide to have a dream about a problem, and decide that the interpretation of the dream will reveal the answer. You must also decide to awaken at the very end of the dream, remember it, and write it down. Just enter your level when you are in bed and ready to go to sleep, and tell yourself mentally that you are going to have a dream, and that you will remember the dream.

The second technique is to decide that the mind will work on a particular problem throughout sleep, and that when you awaken, your first thought will be the answer. At your level, tell yourself that this is what you are going to do. Once you have learned to remember your dreams, it will then be easy to use this technique to program a dream that will help you solve a problem.

I will focus mainly on examples, so you will begin to grasp the magnitude of what programmed dreams enable us to do. Programmed dreams are very valuable, and are well worth the effort to learn.

One of my hospitalized patients, for example, suddenly developed excruciating chest and abdominal pain. The internal medicine specialist thought it might be either a heart attack or a kidney infection. He suggested transferring her to a medical facility. After persuading him to wait until morning, I told the patient, who was a good dreamer, that she had better have a dream that would tell her exactly what it was, where it was, how she got it, why she got it, and exactly what to do.

She also programmed that I would be able to interpret the dream for her, and oddly enough, I immediately knew the interpretation—even though it was highly complex. It is possible that I understood because that is what she programmed.

In her dream, she and her husband were driving along a winding road where they should not have gone when it began to snow. The snow got deeper and deeper, the car veered off the road, and it was covered over with snow. Just beyond where the car went off the road, the road came to a dead end and went into another road at right angles, then into another road at right angles, and then into still another road at right angles. To me this was an anatomical roadmap of the intestinal tract, with an obstruction at the ileocecal junction. But I didn't tell her this. Instead I asked her to draw the roadmap for me. She did, and it even was in correct proportion! The winding road corresponded to the small intestine and the dead end to the cecum. (The three right angles were the ascending, transverse, and descending colon.)

As soon as the car was covered with snow, her husband said, "I have to cut off the engine." The first thing one does for an intestinal obstruction is shut off the fuel supply, the food intake. Then eight or 10 people came from the city to dig them out. Eight or 10 in dreams represents the fingers on two hands, and I did not know if this meant laying on of hands or surgery. When they were dug out, she and her husband were all right, but their three teenage children were gone. They were the reason for the obstruction. She wanted more of her husband's attention for herself.

Intestinal obstruction is an acute surgical emergency, so I immediately transferred her to a surgical hospital. Before she left, I warned her that she needed to have a dream to overcome the obstruction or she'd need surgery.

At the surgical hospital, the diagnosis was confirmed, based on X-ray findings of fluid levels in the gut and blood electrolyte studies. Surgery was scheduled, and she took a nap to program another dream.

In this dream she saw a tall dark man, wearing a turban—as if from the Punjab section of northern India—and he was massaging her abdomen. When she awakened, the obstruction was gone!

To the nondream programmer, these two dreams must sound like something out of *Alice in Wonderland*. But I am only reporting data, and I draw no conclusions about the data.

I further learned that 20 years earlier, a surgeon had performed an operation on this woman for intestinal obstruction. I called the surgeon and asked where in the intestinal tract the obstruction was. He answered that it was the distal portion of the ileum. The ileocecal junction is the distal-most part of the ileum.

SOLVING PROBLEMS WITH PROGRAMMED DREAMS

Programmed dreams can be used to solve any kind of problem, such as problems at work, with children, financial troubles, decisions about whether to get married and other momentous decisions, and so forth. I will stick primarily to medical examples in this brief chapter, and you can learn other applications during the Silva training.

Let me start with one of my own. One time I wrote a very strong letter to a patient who was taking too much Valium. Two nights later during sleep I became aware that she was so infuriated by my letter that she decided to not come back. Then, during sleep, I realized that both of us were at the most telepathic state of consciousness, so I pictured her coming in the next day. When she arrived she said to me, "When I got your letter yesterday I was so peeved that I decided I would never come back. But when I woke up this morning I changed my mind." Of course, she thought that she had changed her mind, but really it was me who put the thought there.

When you program long enough for dreams, the mind becomes aware that you want to gather information during sleep, and it automatically does this for you. The information reaches beyond the dreamer, and beyond information that you would presume is contained in the mind.

One time a dear friend complained about a heart condition that kept recurring. He had balloon dilation of the coronary arteries and also had a stent inserted in an artery, but still he experienced difficulty. I told him about programmed dreams, gave him a set of the dream tapes, and instructed him to wake up with the answer. Two days later I received a call from him. He was at the University of Pennsylvania Medical Center, saying that he had the dream and was told to "get it over with." So he went in for quadruple bypass surgery. I assured him he would not have received the answer if the operation were going to fail, because I had never known a programmed dream to be wrong.

The next night I visited him and learned the surgery already had been completed that morning. During sleep that night, I received a clear message. He was up and running around in my dream, and suddenly one of the arteries burst. The words I heard were "too soon." I knew this was a warning—not that it was *going* to happen, but that it *would* happen if he became active too soon. I cancelled half a day's worth of appointments to go see him and explain the dream. I explained to him that his arteries were made of very delicate 75-year-old tissue, and that he must not get up and rush around too soon—even if his doctors told him it would hasten recovery. His wife and son were there and agreed completely that it would be just like him to be up and dancing practically the next day. It is five years later, and he is alive and well.

I didn't program for the dream and I did not program to awaken with it, and I do not know how it came about—but I was thankful for it.

Note from Ed Bernd Jr.: Techniques for programming dreams are beyond the confines of this brief presentation, but are taught in the basic course, and more information is available on www.DrMcKenzie.com.

This chapter copyrighted by the American Mental Health Association.

Section IV:
Fulfilling Relationships

Chapter 12
ESP for Better Relationships

Good relationships are important in order to make this the happiest time in your life. Higher intelligence will guide and direct you in all aspects of relationships: romantic, marriage and family, children, friends and associates, and business.

We communicate with one another physically, emotionally, and mentally. Besides communicating with other people, we communicate with the very cells that make up life, as Dr. Lipton explained in Chapter 8.

Cleve Backster has been demonstrating what Dr. Lipton talks about for more than 40 years. In 1966, the same year that my father taught his first public "Silva Mind Control" class, Cleve Backster conducted an experiment that changed his life, and changed our way of thinking about the world around us.

PRIMARY PERCEPTION

Backster is a polygraph expert. At the time he had his offices in New York City. Late one night after everyone else had gone home, he decided to conduct an experiment just to see what would happen.

"For whatever reason, it occurred to me that it would be interesting to see how long it took the water to get from the root area of a plant, all the way up the long trunk and out and down to the leaves," he recalled (1995 Silva International Convention, Laredo, Texas).

So he connected the galvanic skin response section of a polygraph onto a leaf of a dracaena plant in his office, poured water into the pot, and sat back to watch and see what happened.

The plant reacted, but not the way Backster expected.

The tracings on the printout had the contour of a human being ,who is being tested, reacting the way a person does when you are asking a question that could get them in trouble.

So I forgot about the rising water time and said to myself, "Wow, this thing wants to show me people-like reactions." So I began to wonder what I could do that would be a threat to the well being of the plant, similar to the fact that a relevant question regarding a crime could be a threat to a person taking a polygraph test if they're lying.

Then the idea occurred to him that he could burn the electroded leaf of the plant. That's when it happened:

I didn't have matches in the room. I wasn't touching the plant in any way. I was maybe five feet away from the desk. I was essentially away from the plant.

The only new thing that occurred was my intent to burn that plant leaf.

In an instant, when I thought of burning that plant leaf and the image entered my mind, the polygraph went into a wild agitation.

Now this was very late at night and towards morning. The building was empty and there was just no other reason for this reaction. I thought, "Wow! It's as though this plant read my mind!" It was that obvious to me right then, and my consciousness hasn't been the same since.

Backster, who now has a laboratory in San Diego, California, has continued to work with what he calls "primary perception." One year, at a Silva International Convention in Laredo, he showed split-screen videos of a woman watching television in her home in San Diego and some of her white cells in a container in Backster's laboratory a couple of miles away.

The electroded cells in the laboratory that had been taken from her body reacted wildly when she saw a scene on the television of a woman being abducted, which is good evidence of what Dr. Lipton said about cells being unique to each person's body.

You can read all about Cleve Backster's research with white cells in the book that he wrote with Dr. Robert B. Stone, *The Secret Life of Your Cells* (Whitford Press 1989). The author, Bob Stone, was another good friend, a Silva instructor for 20 years, and coauthor of several books with my father.

Backster has written his own book, *Primary Perception: Biocommunication with Plants, Living Foods and Human Cells* (Rose Millennium Press 2003). This is the only book written by Backster himself about his four decades of research. You can order through *www.Primaryperception.com* (it is also available at Amazon.com). Or you can order from the Backster Research Foundation, a 501c tax-exempt organization, at 861 Sixth St. #403, San Diego, CA 92101. Author signed copies are available by joining the Bio Web: *www.primaryperception.com/order.html*.

SUBJECTIVE COMMUNICATION

We interact with one another in many ways. We can even influence people remotely, without being in their presence.

There was a research project reported on at a 1972 conference proceeding sponsored jointly by the Mind Science Foundation and Silva International that illustrates this concept. Dr. Bernard Grad, an associate professor of gerontology (the scientific study of the biological, psychological, and sociological phenomena associated with old age and aging) at McGill University School of Medicine, Montreal, Canada, conducted experiments to demonstrate that a healer could cure wounds and illnesses in laboratory mice by the "laying on of hands," transmitting healing energy to the mice.

Dr. Grad also conducted experiments with plants and with seeds. Both were positively affected by the healer's hands.

Then the healer suggested something new to Dr. Grad: If human energy could be stored, it could be saved and used later, so that cells could still be influenced by the human energy even when the human being was no longer there.

Sure enough, the healer could program the water in a positive way, and plants would grow faster. And the healer was not the only one who could do this—so could "average" people.

Dr. Grad even recruited two patients at the mental hospital where he worked to help him. When the container of water was held for a period of time by a psychotically depressed person, the plants watered with that water showed slower growth than those watered with untreated water. When he went to the second patient to ask her if she would participate in his experiment, she was happy to oblige. He explained:

She thought this was a great idea and she brightened right up and this upset me, because I didn't want her to become enthusiastic. In fact, I chose her for the experiment just for the opposite reasons. So there we were and the die was cast and I decided we would just go ahead with the experiment.

When I came back half an hour later she was faithfully holding the bottle, somewhat like a mother holding a child, I thought, in a kind of cradling fashion. I didn't know what to make of all of this but I was going to see what would happen in any case.

I had supposed that this girl's plants would grow more slowly than the control, but this was not so, and I attribute this to the fact that she was quite enthusiastic about the experiment.

The interesting thing is, it is not the diagnosis which is important for this experiment; what is important is the state of mind you are in at the moment.

Water—and other matter—store energy from human beings. Dr. Grad concluded his presentation with the observation that this has major implications for our relationships with one another. "There is the relationship of a mother to cooking," he said. "She has a responsibility there, and I can expand further on this, but time does not allow."

This report goes beyond the scope and space limitations of this chapter, but you can read Dr. Grad's full report on the Website of the Ecumenical Society of Psychorientology (See appendix for Website).

With physical energy, we can help, and we can hurt. You can give someone a helping hand, or you can hit them with your fist—if they are within reach. If they are beyond your reach, then your fist cannot hurt them.

Your words can help or hurt. When someone is within range of your voice, you can say mean things to hurt and upset them. But when they are beyond the range of your voice, you can no longer do that.

When someone is within the reach of the physical part of your aura, then you can use your thoughts to help them or to hurt them. We have all experienced that: Someone comes into the room who is upset and we can sense it immediately. And then there are some people who make everyone feel better as soon as they come into the room.

Harvard social psychology professor Robert Rosenthal is known for his decades of research into self-fulfilling prophecy, experimenter expectancy effects, nonverbal communication, and sources of artifact in data analysis.

In one of his most famous experiments, he selected several laboratory mice at random and told graduate students that they were "maze bright," and he selected other mice and told the students that these were "maze dull." Whether you call it self-fulfilling prophecy of psychosomatic effect or mental projection, the result was that the mice that students thought were smart learned to navigate through the maze much faster than the mice the students thought were dumb.

In one of Rosenthal's more controversial experiments, teachers were told that some students of theirs (chosen at random) were gifted. The result was that those students claimed to be gifted performed better in school.

This provides evidence that we can influence one another for good or ill with our thoughts and emotions when we are within range of the physical part of the aura, about 8 meters (25 feet). Beyond that distance, we can only use the mind to help, we cannot use it to hurt anyone.

You can use your mind to help by reinforcing the signals being sent from higher intelligence. But you cannot use your mind to hurt anyone at a distance. Only physical force can cause physical harm. If the person is beyond your reach (beyond the reach of your fist or the sound of your voice or the physical part of your aura), you cannot hurt them.

If someone believes that you can harm them with your thoughts, then they may harm themselves psychosomatically, but you cannot force it on them. Anyone who understands and believes that negative thoughts and negative suggestions have no influence over them will never suffer any harm no matter what anybody thinks of them. That is why we repeat that statement over and over again in our conditioning cycles.

MENTAL PROJECTION TO
IMPROVE RELATIONSHIPS

We are involved in all kinds of relationships: family, social friends, and business associates. There are parent-child relationships, employer-employee relationships, and doctor-patient relationships, as well as relationships between salesperson and customer, and many more.

You can use your Everyday ESP to detect information that can help you to troubleshoot all kinds of relationship problems, even before they develop. You can learn to sense the other person's needs and wants so that you can respond appropriately.

You can use Everyday ESP to detect the invisible barriers that people have erected, old wounds you may have forgotten, or not even know about, and misunderstandings that have never been adequately resolved. Then you can use remote influencing to establish rapport at deep, inner levels, and watch the changes that take place at the outer level.

That's what Marie Buckingham (now Burleson) did. Shortly after completing the Silva training, she found herself faced with a challenge in a junior-high school classroom.

There were four troublemakers in one of her classes, four girls who disrupted the rest of the students so that no one could participate. It was not limited to just Marie's classroom. These same girls had a reputation among the faculty and the school counselor for causing similar trouble in all of their classes.

For one week, Marie programmed herself to wake up earlier than usual so she could project to these girls while they were still asleep. Here's Marie's story, in her own words:

I would get up, maybe 15 minutes early, and project each one on my mental screen. I'd spend five minutes, maybe less, on each one. I told them that it's more fun to be good than bad and reminded each one that I thought she was a wonderful person.

And they were all nice girls, and they were all intelligent.

I told them that I hoped they would cooperate in class so that they, and their classmates and I, could all enjoy the class. I told them I looked forward to having them do this and that I would appreciate it. Then I thanked them.

After the next class, I asked them to stay behind for a minute. I told them that they were creating problems in the class, but that I knew they were nice people.

When they came to class the next time, the ringleader refused to let herself become involved in the antics of the other three. She sat apart from them.

During the next class, she asked a question. The other students looked at her in disbelief. Pretty soon, though, she came up with some ideas, and by the end of class, all four girls were participating in class.

As they left the room at the end of class, the ringleader looked at me, smiled, and said, "You know, I think it's more fun being good than bad."

That was the end of my trouble with the troublemakers.

Imagine how valuable these skills are for parents. There will be people in your child's peer group wanting him to join a gang. Somebody is going to try to get one of your children to try drugs. Four of his friends will be there, calling him "chicken" and trying to get him to try it. How important will your powers of Remote Influencing be at that instant? How valuable will they be? Now is the time to practice and develop your ability.

Somebody is going to pressure your teenage daughter to try sex—unprotected sex. This could be a life-and-death decision that you are making today when you decide to develop your Everyday ESP.

You can use Remote Influencing to reach your children at a deep inner level where they know you are telling them the truth, that what you are telling them really is in their best interest, just as Marie Buckingham did.

USING OTHER PEOPLE'S EXPERIENCES

You can detect information that has been impressed on your own brain neurons. That's called "memory." Your mind can retrieve the information that has been stored in your "memory banks." You can use all of the facts that you have accumulated in your "memory banks" to provide insight, and to help you make decisions.

You can also use all of the experiences that you have accumulated and stored on your brain neurons to help you make decisions about your future actions.

You can also detect information that has been stored on other people's brain neurons. You can do *more* than detect the facts stored on someone else's brain neurons; you can also learn how that person applied that information, and the results he or she got. In other words, you can learn from their experiences, and then apply them to your own situation. This, my father said, is wisdom: using other people's experiences as if they were your own.

Even though my father has been gone for several years, we still call on him for help. It is amazing how many ideas come to us after we go to level and use the MentalVideo to obtain guidance about decisions we have to make concerning the business that he left to us. We have been guided to information that we never knew existed, and have developed successful strategies and plans that we sure didn't think up ourselves.

EXAMPLES OF EVERYDAY ESP

IN RELATIONSHIPS

Now let's look at some more real-life examples to give you some ideas and insight as to how *you* can use Everyday ESP to improve *your* relationships. Let's start with a medical doctor and how Everyday ESP helped him to deal with the stresses of a hectic medical practice.

"Something seems to be happening," obstetrician Calvin Poole, M.D., of Gloster, Mississippi, said after obtaining Jose Silva's UltraMind ESP System home-study course. "I am not sure what it is, but luck seems to be improving and the daily worries don't seem to be getting to me, such as under-staffing and problems with interactions between staff and patients.

"I even heard the comment that I looked happier than I had in a long time," he continued. One of the problems he was dealing with was severe injuries from an accident. "Headaches are almost gone, too," he said. "I am rapidly getting sold on the UltraMind System, as you can probably tell, which would also explain my eagerness in finding a seminar to take.

"One other thing that I have noticed is that I seem to have more endurance than I have had since the accident two years ago. I do contribute that to the System. The brain power seems to be back to normal.

"As always," he added, "feel free to use any comments, and I will be glad to field any questions and give the highest recommendations to the Silva UltraMind System. I still intend to be an instructor. Like I said, I don't know *how* it works, but it does."

Since writing those comments, Dr. Poole has indeed become a Silva instructor. His contact information is in the Appendix.

A graduate in Italy named Daniele used the MentalVideo Technique to improve relationships for people on an Internet mailing list. The results came quickly, and conformed to the Laws of Programming by benefitting "two or more people."

I'm within a mailing list where all people are badmouthing about all. I used the MentalVideo and I create a new list where all help others and the participants are happy to subscribe in this list.

After a few hours, the people on the list started a new thread where all share their ideas with joy and happiness. Do you think this is caused by my MentalVideo?

BETTER FAMILY RELATIONSHIPS

Our friend Dolores, who works in the high-tech industry in the northwestern United States, sent us these examples of family relationships:

A close relative and I hadn't talked with each other for over two years because of some nasty disagreement we had last time we had a family function. I was finally going to make a trip all the way across the country to go visit long-lost family and I knew there was no way to avoid him, which is what I really wanted to do, so I programmed ahead of time that when I saw him we would resolve our differences. I didn't know how, but I had the desire to resolve things. It wasn't doing me any good holding onto hard feelings.

I felt that this would be a really good test of the methods for me because it really did seem like an impossible situation. So I went to level and did the 3-Scenes Technique:

First scene I showed the conflict we had had last time I was with him at the family function. I presented it in all its grand detail and glory, complete with emotions and every visual detail I could remember.

Second scene I mentally pictured the two of us together, sitting, actually talking in a civilized friendly manner, including emotion and visual details, certain people present, etc.

Third scene, we were laughing, joking with each other, a strong feeling of friendliness surrounding us, then parting with a big warm hug.

Now what's interesting is that I had forgotten about that program until now—two and a half weeks later. What actually happened is almost exactly like what I had programmed for, right down to the hug. This relative and I are actually talking again and on friendly terms.

Just the other day I did a 3-Scenes Technique for a "project" I had in mind. Within minutes of completing the three scenes I received a phone call from someone I hadn't heard from in a long time, and it was related to what I had just programmed for. That kind of thing happens a lot with the 3-Scenes Technique. Sometimes it's quick (that time was exceptionally quick). Other times an indication might not happen for a few hours or a day.

I have recently started practicing going to an open-eyes level so that I can see auras and chakras. I consider that a remote viewing method. Might be considered an advanced method, but Jose Silva said that with time and practice we would find ourselves going to level as needed automatically, with eyes either open or closed.

PARENTS AND CHILDREN

Parents have a special bond with their children, especially the mother. The child was once part of the mother, part of her body, and a subjective connection remains throughout their lives.

This was demonstrated in a research project when a mother rabbit was separated from her babies and they were killed one at a time, at random intervals. A response was measured in the mother rabbit's brain at the exact moment each of her babies was killed.

This natural connection between parent and child can be used to help the child. Here is a wonderful example that we just received from a medical doctor in Cairo, Egypt, Dr. Dr Hani Badr. Dr. Badr has been learning the Silva Method from a home study course. Here is what he wrote to us:

My 5 year old daughter complained of a sudden onset of intermittent abdominal pain, which did not respond to symptomatic medicines. During the attack she was crying and straining. I realized that the situation needed investigation so we began with ultrasound which revealed that one portion of the bowel had slid into the next (like the pieces of a telescope) creating an obstruction in the bowel, a serious childhood medical emergency called "Intussusception," which if not reversed will cause damage to the intestine.

I consulted a trusted surgeon. He advised admitting her to the hospital to evaluate surgical intervention. During that time I tried to do something. I put my hand on her abdomen while at alpha, prayed, and imagined some sort of healing power traveling from my mind through my hand to her abdomen.

On reaching the hospital the pain had nearly subsided and on repeating the examinations, her abdomen was almost free and the telescoped segment has resolved.

We know that medicine is not merely chemical drugs, but mind and faith are the cornerstone of health after God's will.

BETTER BUSINESS RELATIONSHIPS

Joanne Larkins of Storrs, Connecticut, used the Instant Rapport Technique that is in the UltraMind ESP System home-study course. With that technique, you program yourself to wake up automatically during the night at the best time to program. Then, when you wake up, you sit up in bed and program to have instant rapport with a client you are going to meet with the next day. Here is her report of her experiences:

I am an astrologer, as well as a full-time homemaker, wife, and mother, and a client was due to come the next day. Here is what happened, from my notes:

I did the Instant Rapport Technique before I went to sleep with the message that I will awake when my client will be ready to meet mentally. I dreamed that I was at an entrance to hotel, and I was apparently waiting for someone. It dawned on me in my dream that this was my clue that I needed to wake up to program my coming session with my client.

So I woke up, sat up on my bed, and proceeded to have the imaginary session with my client, giving my client the assurance that what I did in the consultation would be helpful and that I would help, so that the client could trust me.

Indeed the consultation went exceedingly well, only too long.

There is an extra challenge, in my opinion, to people, mostly women who have chosen the path as home manager, wife, and stay-at-home mom, with this type of program. There is enormous tension because in my choosing to give to all in my household, there is a trade-off, and some sacrifice to those talents that are mine.

Maybe this is only an excuse, however, and on the positive side, the one phrase, "Negative thoughts and negative suggestions have no influence over me at any level of my mind," has freed me in so many ways. It has helped to begin my own turnaround, at the tender age of 53.

After we read her story, we pointed out to her that the MentalVideo is easier to use, and more effective. For one thing, you don't have to wake up during the night and do the programming, you take care of it before you go to sleep.

In addition, you do not have to figure out all the details yourself. Higher intelligence will help you. When you create your MentalVideo, just indicate how much time you have available, and your tutor will find some way to help keep the session shorter. And higher intelligence can also help you balance the many tasks you have undertaken. Joanne is now working with the MentalVideo Technique.

SENSE OF HUMOR

Does higher intelligence have a sense of humor? You can decide for yourself after you read this experience, sent to us by C.J. McGaughey of Norcross, Georgia:

I would like to get your opinion of a very sensitive issue that I was dealing with when I initially began the Silva UltraMind System home study course back in November of last year.

At the time, I was asking for guidance as to how to deal with a relationship with a friend whom I thought did not have my best interests at heart. I forgave the friend for his actions using the following technique:

I called up my friend in my mind's eye and surrounded him with a white light and wished him a life of peace, wealth, and happiness. I then let the image go and smiled. I actually felt great!

A couple weeks later I was clearing out a folder that had personal letters and cards from friends and family. Because I had received a phone call, I hurriedly place the manila folder on my bathroom counter adjacent to the toilet. After finishing my phone call, I retrieved the folder; however, the contents of the folder ended up all over my bathroom floor with the exception of one letter, which went directly in the toilet. This letter was from the friend whom I had forgiven. I did not know what to make of the situation back in December, so I decided it was best to let the friendship go.

Therefore, I did not pursue contact with the individual until recently (a week ago). For whatever reason, I am getting the same negative vibes from this individual. Can you please let me know what you think of this situation?

I apologize for the long e-mail, but there are not many people with whom I can share this situation.

We replied that it sounds to us as if somebody is trying to tell him that the relationship is in the toilet.

Now let's close with a serious story about someone who found the kind of new long-term relationship of which she had always dreamed.

DEMONSTRATE WHAT KIND OF PERSON YOU ARE

A friend of mine who recently found her ideal mate is an excellent example. Katherine Handorf used to work for us here in our Laredo headquarters, and is now the owner of Avlis Productions, a company that promotes our work. When she was younger she made some terrible choices, starting with a man who beat her badly. She finally got away from him and "moved up" to men who only abused her emotionally, not physically.

She programmed for guidance—she thinks of it as praying. Her associate and my coauthor, Ed Bernd Jr., was also using the MentalVideo to help obtain guidance from higher intelligence so that she would find the right person—if he existed. And she got wonderful guidance. Sometimes we had to help her analyze and understand it.

For instance, she prayed to find out if a man she had been dating was serious about her. She e-mailed him and asked him if he wanted to get together and do something that weekend. He e-mailed her back and said he wanted to get away by himself for the weekend and think about his life and what he wanted for the future.

"What does that mean?" she asked.

"It means just what it says," Ed told her. "It means that he is making decisions about his future and you are not involved."

After a couple of days, she finally accepted the fact that it meant that his thoughts about the future didn't include her. And she moved on.

Eventually her intuition guided her to a church (she had never belonged to a church before), and she found a singles group there that was perfect for her. It served as a wonderful support group for her. She was very active, contributing a lot to the group, and benefitting greatly from it.

She continued dating, but without expectations. "If the right one comes along, that's great," she said, "but I'm not expecting it." We continued including her in our MentalVideos, too.

She joined the local volunteer fire department, as one more way to do something to help her community. And when the associate pastor at the church, Lance, who was the advisor to the singles group, asked her to help him out with his high school class reunion, she readily agreed. He was from a town a couple of hundred miles away from where she lived in Austin, Texas.

However, the church decided they were short of money, so they laid Lance off. He quickly found a job in another state. Later, when it was time for his high school class reunion, Lance e-mailed Kathy and asked if she was still planning to come to his old hometown and help him.

"I didn't really want to," she recalled, "I was working hard, and was preparing to go to the Fire Fighters Academy for a week, but Lance is a good man who tries to help people, so I told him I'd be there."

Meanwhile, one of Lance's high school classmates, who still lives in their hometown, was also reluctant to go. But some of his friends encouraged him to attend, so he did. Kathy noticed him, just standing around, so as she sat there at the registration table next to Lance, Kathy asked, "Who's that guy over there, in the cowboy hat?" (She likes cowboys).

Lance told her that was one of his classmates, David. She went over and introduced herself to David. They hit it off immediately, and Kathy stayed a couple of extra days to get to know David better. The next weekend David came to Austin to visit Kathy. The following weekend she went to visit him. After a few weekends of that, Kathy decided to move. She got an apartment, and saw David every day.

They were married in March 2005, with Lance officiating. He thinks that he is the one responsible for bringing his old classmate and his best friend Kathy together. In a way he is, because he was used by higher intelligence to get Kathy to the right place at the right time.

Kathy has always wanted to be in a loving relationship, and now she is. Isn't it interesting that all those years she tried and tried, all she got was heartache and grief (not to mention bruises and concussions)?

Then when she began to focus on finding out what higher intelligence wants her to do with her life, and taking action to help people, to correct problems, and to improve conditions wherever and however she could, "all else was added unto her."

"Seek ye first the kingdom of heaven," she learned the Silva course 15 years ago, and she prayed for guidance from "the Lord," to use her terminology. We use the term "higher intelligence."

"Function within God's righteousness." Even while working full time, and later with her own home business, she still found time to help those who asked, without reservation, without judgment. She gave rides to those who needed them, she brought people into her apartment when they needed a place to stay, and she was the first to volunteer to help with church activities.

And she kept dating and waiting to see if she'd ever find someone. Yes, she wanted to find someone, but she also realized that if it was not meant to be, then she'd continue on with her life and do what she could to make the world a better place to live.

"And all else shall be added unto you." Was that one last test from higher intelligence, to go and help a friend when it was inconvenient and she didn't particularly want to do it? Or was it just a part of the totality of her life, that made it easier for higher intelligence to bring the two of them together?

My Uncle Juan Silva told us about the time that he and my father were experimenting to see if they could program Juan to be an inventor. They had done their programming, and Juan was sitting, thinking, waiting for something "to come" to him when his stepfather pulled him up out of the chair and shoved him toward the machine shop they had and told him to get to work.

Juan started turning a rod on a lathe, just to be doing something. Then he noticed that he was creating a "rack gear." And then the thought came to him: a rack gear was the perfect thing to use to operate a vending machine for use in Mexico. He got his invention, and it earned him a lot of money.

"Once you get up and get into action and start moving around," he told us, "there's a much better chance that the solution will bump into you."

That's exactly what happened with Kathy. She was up moving around, doing things. She was "functioning within God's righteousness," so she was being noticed by higher intelligence. When the opportunity presented itself, higher intelligence got Kathy and David together.

If she had just been thinking of herself, rather than doing the things that higher intelligence sent her here to do, then higher intelligence wouldn't have been paying attention to her, it would have been busy with someone else who was doing the work it wanted done.

My father's research—and a lifetime of experience—convinced him that life is not made up of a bunch of isolated incidents. And it is not about how to make ourselves happy.

"We were sent here for a purpose," he said. And when we are striving to fulfill that purpose, then "all else shall be added unto us."

That's why the very last thing we say in the course each day, the final statement, used at the very end of the last conditioning cycle that we use each day, says:

"You will continue to strive to take part in constructive and creative activities to make this a better world to live in, so that when you move on, you will have left behind a better world for those who follow.

"You will consider the whole of humanity, depending on their ages, as father or mothers, brothers or sisters, sons or daughters.

"You are a superior human being; you have greater understanding, compassion, and patience with others."

Notice that you are not required to succeed at every effort you make—nobody does. But you are expected to continue to make every effort you can to improve conditions on the planet—without any expectation of compensation. Your needs will be met. Maybe you'll give far more than you receive—so what! Your needs will be met.

These are new and different ideas from what we've been taught in the past. Not everyone understands them, not everyone accepts them. We submit them for your consideration; the choice is yours.

If you want to do it yourself, then go to your level and visualize what you want.

If you want your life to have meaning, then follow my father's favorite formula:

Seek ye first the kingdom of heaven, function within God's righteousness, and all else shall be added unto you.

Best wishes in your quest.

Chapter 13
Love and Energy Fields
by Jose Silva

(A few years ago, my father found a handwritten manuscript containing thoughts he had jotted down several years earlier, and passed it on to us. It gives considerable insight and is extremely valuable information for everyone who is in love, or who wants to be. Here it is, just the way he wrote it. Keep in mind that my parents were happily married for more than 50 years and raised 10 children.)

It is interesting to note that when researchers are researching in a specific field, some stumble onto bits of interesting information related to other fields. This is a report about such an observation.

When investigating a lead, a researcher often uncovers information that borders on other important fields. The particular area of interest in this case has to do with love and energy fields.

Thirty years of research in the area of the mind, through which the Silva Method was conceived, have taken us to many places; we have interviewed and investigated many people of both sexes, varying ages, many cultures, races, and creeds.

On one occasion I would find myself face to face with people who performed with what I considered to be prophetic wisdom. Some of these people, when relating their information, did not seem to make too much sense as perceived from a certain point of view. But from a different perspective the same information appears prophetic and carries great wisdom.

It appears that many years of research and experience are needed to develop the required factors that help the researcher reach his ideal baseline from which he can perceive prophetic wisdom with greater sensitivity.

To report these findings to you, the reader, the information has been arranged in an order that I thought would make the most sense. Because all this information has been compiled from the wise and prophetic sayings of so many individuals when at their wisest point in time, the title given this report is:

WISDOM SPEAKS

From here on, every time reference is made to any of the individuals interviewed or investigated, I will refer to their wisdom, saying, "Wisdom said..." or, "Wisdom thought..." and so forth. But keep in mind, this is not from only one person; it is the combined and agreed-upon wisdom of many wise people who shared their experience and insight.

"Wisdom Speaks" is the compilation of information of many individuals who, because of their experience, arrived at some conclusions or assumptions concerning a particular subject. Some of these subjects have not been researched by conventional scientific methods, and some may not be researched by conventional scientific methods for a long time.

It is interesting to note that all of these individuals who contributed information arrived at their conclusions or assumptions on their own, without knowing that others in the past had arrived at the same conclusions; or better still, that others would in the future arrive at the same conclusions.

Before we enter our main subject, "Wisdom speaks about love and energy fields," let us review important basic principles offered to us by Wisdom.

CONCEPTS OF WISDOM

Wisdom refers to God or Creator as High Intelligence, and states that creation of the Universe has not been completed, that it is still in an evolving process toward peak perfection. Wisdom agrees that human beings, with human intelligence, are representatives of High Intelligence at the planetary plane of existence level.

Wisdom explains that the mission of the human being on this planet is to become aware of and remove all opposing forces that hinder the flow of the evolving process of creation as it moves toward peak perfection. This is known as problem-solving.

Wisdom also acknowledges the programming power of High Intelligence to program energy at all planes of existence, such as the spiritual, sub-atomic, atomic, molecular, cellular, organ, and organ system. Energy and its field of radiation together have governing power in molding things according to environmental needs.

Wisdom has said that all human beings who have landed on this planet, and are on their own personal journey while functioning as husbands, wives, fathers, mothers, sons, or daughters, have landed here to help High Intelligence make this planet a better world to live in through problem-solving.

Every human being arrives on the planet alone, is here for a short stay, and leaves alone, resuming the universal journey.

Wisdom says that all inhabitants of this planet, regardless of their race, creed, religion, or intelligence, leave this planet in a period of approximately 100 years, to be replaced by newcomers arriving on the planet. Wisdom's concept of High Intelligence is that the highest intelligence of all is in charge of the whole Universe; that a lesser intelligence is in charge of a group of galaxies; and a still lesser intelligence is in charge of our galaxy.

Wisdom is convinced that the High Intelligence in charge of our solar system, our planet, and us, does not watch over us or our planet every second of the day in order to help us or our planet. Wisdom believes that High Intelligence automatically tunes into our planet in cycles of so many years. The same holds true for individual human beings, Wisdom feels.

There is only one other way for this attunement with High Intelligence to take place, Wisdom says. That is for the majority of the inhabitants of this planet to jointly enter a special dimension of the mind and jointly ask for help. Otherwise, Wisdom believes that channels have been created to which the human being can become attuned to seek and get help when help is needed for taking care of creation. Wisdom also believes that the urge to mate and conceive is due to fundamental programming by High Intelligence. This programming establishes marriage and conception of children as the system selected by High Intelligence to continue placing more inhabitants on this planet.

Wisdom says that the primary purpose for humans on this planet is for making this planet a better world to live in; everything else is secondary. So, married or not, or married but with no children, the obligation of the human being remains the same: primarily to help make this planet a better place to live.

Wisdom says the so-called population explosion would not exist if every human being was on the job making this planet a better world to live in. Wisdom believes there is a balancing mechanism that automatically adjusts the planet's population in relation to the amount of work done by each human being. This adjustment would match the expected annual progress to the flow of the evolving process of creation that is taking place throughout our galaxy.

So, Wisdom says, as more work is done per human being to catch up with the expected progress of this planet, then fewer humans will be placed on this planet due to the automatic system created by High Intelligence.

The information discussed so far is valuable in helping us center our minds so as to function from a superior perspective and perceive information with greater understanding.

WISDOM SPEAKS ABOUT LOVE
AND ENERGY FIELDS

Wisdom believes that a specific compounded state of chemistry existing under a special set of environmental conditions is what allows a field of life-giving energy to be transferred from the spiritual dimension into the biological dimension. This is what we know as conception.

In the case of conception of a human being, the life-giving energy field serves as a mold that influences biological growth and development to conform to a human body. Once the body is formed, other energy fields come into being. These include energy fields caused by activity at the sub-atomic, atomic, molecular, cellular, organ, and organ system functioning levels.

The life-giving energy field that found its way through the chemistry from the spiritual dimension into the biological dimension is the basic fundamental life-giving energy field. All of the other energy fields are artifact due to biological functioning.

Finally, a very complex aura of interlaced, interlocked energy fields is established, and surrounds the human body. Wisdom says that this aura that surrounds the human body is vibrating in a manner and at a rate influenced by the sum total of all influencing factors.

The influence from the genetic dimension is such a factor, according to Wisdom. Wisdom believes that all experiences of all our ancestors have also been transferred from parent to child at the genetic level. Other influencing factors include the heavenly bodies that influence matter, affecting the human being from conception on; our own environmental, psychological, and physiological experiences; and the influence caused on us by the projected thoughts of others.

All of these contributed influences cause the human aura to vibrate at the rate that it does. Keep in mind that the human aura is composed of several energy fields, each vibrating at its own rate.

When boy meets girl—or better still, when boy sees girl and girl sees boy—if their auras are somewhat compatible, they will experience a body chemistry change because they like what they see. Wisdom says that a body chemistry change is accompanied by an aura vibration rate change.

Wisdom knows that the aura of every human being, male or female, is different from every other human aura. Wisdom also knows that when male and female see each other and like what they see, the aura of each starts changing in a direction to be more compatible with the other.

The next thing that will happen to the male and female in question is to get close to each other to talk. At this point, the sense of hearing comes into play, causing a greater chemical change, which in turn causes a greater degree of change in the rate of aura vibration. This change of vibration is now assured of being in the direction of increased compatibility because when bodies are close to one another their auras are touching and interlaced with one another.

Next is the sense of touch. Each desires to touch the other, bringing about a still greater change in the auras toward a greater compatibility.

At this point, Wisdom directs our attention to notice what is happening to two individuals who each possessed a very personal and unique aura, different from any other aura possessed by anybody else on this planet. What is happening, of course, is that the auras of these individuals are changing toward the establishment of new and different rates of aura vibration brought about by the combined effects of two auras. These new rates of vibration will still be different from the vibration rates of any other auras.

Maximum change of aura toward compatibility will take place when an exchange of body chemistry between the male and female is effected.

To maintain aura compatibility, Wisdom says that we need to reinforce the factors known to maintain compatibility. These factors are:

o   Closeness of the physical bodies.

o   Speaking frequently.

o   Touching each other.

o   Participation in the exchange of body chemistry through kissing and the sex act.

Wisdom has said that to maintain reinforced aura compatibility is to maintain reinforced love between husband and wife. Aura compatibility and love between husband and wife are weakened when their bodies are kept distant from one another, and when there is no body chemistry exchange taking place between the two.

Wisdom recommends the following for the maintenance of strong love ties between husband and wife:

1. Maintain frequent close-range verbal contact.

2. Practice frequent body contact.

3. Practice kissing at every opportunity.

4. Practice the sex act as frequently as possible.

5. Do not sleep in separate rooms or in separate beds; sleep in the same bed.

Wisdom guarantees that when husband and wife comply with the five indicated steps, a strong love bond will be maintained that nothing except the power of God can separate.

This strong love bond is established through aura compatibility reinforcement.

WORDS FROM WISDOM

Remember husband, you were created to do everything within your power to make your wife happy first, and yourself second.

Remember wife, you were created to do everything within your power to make your husband happy first, and yourself second.

When the words of Wisdom are practiced, happiness is guaranteed for husband and wife.

Have a happy married life.

Wisdom.

Chapter 14
Creating a Genius
by Jose Silva

You can begin creating your genius child even before conception.

You and your mate, both having learned my ESP System, are both clairvoyant. You have discussed having a child, and you agree that this child you are planning to have shall be a genius.

You now need to use your clairvoyant ability to look ahead 15 years to see what skill will help the world the most.

If your child is a genius in mathematical skills, such skills may no longer be needed in the light of a computerized society. You need to use your clairvoyance to look ahead 15 years (remotely view into the future), and pinpoint critical professions. Why 15 years? Because your genius will be educated in special ways, so that by the time he or she is 15, education will be accomplished to the doctorate level, and your genius will be ready to enter the workforce.

Will this be a critical time in terms of world diplomacy? In world health? In business? Your genius will be in the right place at the right time with the right skills. You and your mate are in possession of the controls. Here is how to use them:

You need to use these controls separately. You need to enter your center—the 10 cycles alpha level—at the same time but at a sufficient distance apart so that you do not influence each other's results.

Papa and mama need to be separated from one another by a distance greater than 100 feet. This is so the body's radiated energy fields are not in contact with one another physically.

The two of you might very well come to the same conclusion about the kind of specialist that will be needed in 15 years. However, there are a number of critical jobs to do on earth at any one moment in time, and these two clairvoyants might tap into different ones. They must then try again. This time they might ask for a number of priorities and see later where they overlap.

Let's suppose that they both concluded that more medical doctors will be needed. Then papa and mama now know that they need to conceive a medical doctor.

The next step is for papa and mama to enter the clairvoyant level (their center) together. Once at their center, they talk to each other about conceiving a medical doctor. They discuss the pros and cons. They converse about the area of expertise.

Once they are in agreement, they both start working together, cooperating, in selecting the features that the child would have.

Mama might suggest that she would like for her son or daughter to have blue eyes like her grandfather. Papa might describe what hair his son or daughter would have.

This may seem to be irrelevant to the genius factor, but it is quite relevant to the offspring factor. The parents-to-be will be programming both for a genius and for an infant that will be compatible, an infant that will fit into the family in every way.

They should not try to select the sex of the child, but let the selection be done by higher intelligence. The intelligence that resides on the other side, where we came from and where we go back to when we die, controls the entire Universe. It will make the selection, and keep the proper balance of males and females on the planet.

It is said that basically humans, and some animals, satisfy their mating needs with only one partner. In times when only the males went to war and millions were killed, the majority of conceptions were males, to bring the population back into balance. The balance of males to females stays close to 50-50 in normal times. That means one male for one female. If we change this male to female balance, we get into trouble. So do not try to select the sex.

Both parents should also be spending some related time daily imagining the genius offspring functioning as a successful, clairvoyant, mature adult. What is different about a clairvoyant physician or healthcare practitioner? Mentally picture the genius that is about to be conceived functioning in the following ways.

- o The clairvoyant doctor can diagnose at a distance without even talking to the patient and be more correct than most doctors are today. Furthermore, a clairvoyant doctor can heal at a distance, be more accurate in prescribing medication, and avoid the temptation of high professionals fees in deciding for or against surgery.

- o A clairvoyant physician who practices psychiatry can project into patient's dreams or hallucinations to analyze the problem. This physician can, from a distance, mentally regress the patient to find the root of the problem.

The following are mental images that both parents should be enjoying daily while relaxed, once they have selected the occupation and physical looks of their genius soon to be conceived.

- o If the occupation decided upon was diplomat or other positions of government leadership, mentally picture the clairvoyant diplomat or government in action. He or she is able to project into the future (remotely view the future), and detect what the needs of the people will be so that they can be ready when that need arrives.

- o Will your genius be a law enforcement officer? As a clairvoyant, he or she will be able to go back in time (remotely view the past) to know the details of a crime, to know how to identify and take into custody all criminals who are violating the Creator's work.

- o Will your genius be an engineer? Clairvoyant petroleum engineers and geologists can dowse for minerals and resources without the use of a divining rod. They can know how deep the oil or other minerals are plus their quantity and quality. Uri Geller, a psychic genius, left the entertainment stage and, in a few short years, made a fortune using his clairvoyant abilities in this way.

- o Will your genius be an industrialist? Then daydream about him or her manufacturing the very products that will be in demand, and doing so in an efficient, cost-effective way.

o The clairvoyant executive will be able to neutralize stress, maintain health, and select exactly the right people for the right jobs. Then decisions will be uncannily accurate. Financiers will multiply funds like magic, and will put those funds back to work to improve conditions on the planet.

o Clairvoyant farmers and ranchers are able to work with nature in intuitive ways that defy logical reasoning. Crops flourish, weather conditions are foreseen and prepared for, even artificial insemination has a higher percentage of takes, making for a more economical venture.

So, there is a period of time when you both, as parents-to-be of a genius, daydream about the future accomplishments of your clairvoyant offspring.

We humans have a very big responsibility, not only to become geniuses ourselves, to become clairvoyants so that we can correct problems, and make better decisions and prevent problems; we must also teach our children. We need to become geniuses ourselves and we need to create other geniuses, if we are to be as our Creator intended us to be.

So you must not only create genius in yourself (which you are doing by learning the UltraMind ESP System), you must also create a genius in your forthcoming child, and you must also encourage your family, your neighbors, and your business associates to also learn to use the right brain hemisphere, to develop their ESP, and to become geniuses. You need to set the world on fire with your genius.

I want you to think of this before you go to bed, because the more excited you are at the prospect of creating a genius, the more quickly you are likely to conceive.

Every cell in your body knows your thoughts and feelings. The woman's reproductive system responds. The male reproductive system responds. Both reproductive systems are honored to be given one of the Creator's top priorities: to make planet earth a better place to live.

You are now both ready to consummate the sex act. The wife is now ready to conceive.

When you think that the education of your genius child should be-gin? It should begin as soon as you know there is a pregnancy. Enter your level and talk to your unborn child.

HOW TO TEACH YOUR CHILDREN TO USE ESP

You can use the following information, whether you are a Silva graduate or not, if you are starting to train your children at age 7. This information is essential in teaching children to become geniuses.

1. Explain to the child what visualization is and how to practice visualization.

2. Explain to the child what imagination is and how to practice imagination.

Visualization with the left brain is the ability to mentally recall what something looks like after an impression has been made on the left brain hemisphere at 20 cycles per second beta, using the sense of sight and with eyes focused.

Visualization with the right brain is the ability to mentally picture a previous impression made on the right brain hemisphere at 10 cycles per second brain frequency, through subjective communication.

Imagination with the left brain is the ability to alter what exists to obtain better results.

Imagination with the right brain is the ability to create something for the first time, something that did not exist on our planet previously.

The ideal age of the child to work with is between 7 and 14, during the second seven-year anabolic life cycle.

During this anabolic life cycle, the child gets a new set of teeth. The male's voice changes to a mature voice and the female begins her monthly rhythm.

The mind of both males and females start functioning deductively. That means that they develop the ability to analyze problems and fig-ure out solutions.

The overall average predominant brain frequency of a child be-tween ages 7 and 14, when eyes are closed or defocused and rolled slightly upward, is between 7 and 14 cycles per second, centering on 10 cycles per second.

PROCEDURE

VISUALIZATION

Get the child to practice visualization by closing the eyes, rolling them slightly upward in relation to the face, and recalling and describing in full detail and color, people, places, and things that they have seen. This should be done for 15 minutes, once a week, preferably on Sunday.

Get the child to explain what they have seen on television or at a movie. The child should explain the movie in full detail and color with eyes closed and turned slightly upward. They are not to explain the plot, but to describe what they saw, what it looked like, in full detail and color.

On the last Sunday of each month (we will assume you are practicing on Sunday), tell the child to practice imagination.

With the eyes closed and rolled upward slightly, the child should alter any images they have seen. For instance, if the child has seen someone with a green sweater, then mentally change that sweater to red, and create a mental picture of the same person wearing a red sweater. The child could imagine that person entering his or her home and coming out wearing a red sweater instead of a green one.

This kind of practice—practicing visualization for 15 minutes for the first three (or sometimes four) Sundays and practicing imagination on the last Sunday—should be continued for one year. Start when the child turns 7 years of age and continue until he or she is 8.

Then when the child is 8, practice every other Sunday until the child turns 9.

After that, practice on one Sunday, then skip two Sundays. Continue this schedule until the child turns 10.

After that, practice one Sunday, then skip three Sundays. Continue this until the child becomes 11.

Thereafter, practice once a month until the child becomes 14 years of age.

CASE WORKING

When the child reaches eight years of age, by this time they have practiced visualization for one year. The parents, who have developed their own clairvoyant ability through the Silva training, or who have trained themselves for 40 days, should then introduce the child to case working, as practiced in the Silva Method and as outlined in this book.

From the age of 11 to the age of 14, the child should practice case working as well as practice visualization.

This is the natural way for children to develop their clairvoyant ability.

Once they have developed this ability to communicate subjectively, they will receive many benefits:

- o They can communicate subjectively with their body and keep it healthy.

- o They can communicate subjectively with other people and avoid conflicts, and obtain information they can use to solve problems.

- o They can communicate subjectively with higher intelligence on the other side, and get guidance and help to correct any problem.

Do this for your child, and they will not need to take the Silva training.

Remember, both graduate and non-graduate parents can train their own children between the ages of 7 and 14 and never have to send them to the course.

And parents who are graduates can go further than that: they can attract the genius they desire.

The child should also be given cases to do daily. These should be health cases to start with, as these are the easiest to do. Later, you can give business, political, social, or personal problems as cases.

The reason that health cases are the easiest for all of us to do is because human survival is our mind's number one priority. It is easiest to be clairvoyant when the problem is related to life and death.

Similarly, the hardest projects are those that are irrelevant to survival, problems that nobody is worrying about (such as, will it rain three years from today?). Every case should involve a meaningful problem of some sort. The mind does not want to waste time on situations that are not problems. The more a person is concerned or affected by a problem, or the more a person is suffering or is life-threatened by a problem, the better the problem is for the child to work on at this stage.

It would be inadvisable to refer now to psychic ability or clairvoyance. Children do not like to be different from their peers. They do not hear other children talk about psychic ability, the psi factor, or clairvoyance, so their motivation could be impaired.

But all children enjoy guessing. Guessing is acceptable. So doing cases become guessing, and the child is measured in "guessing ability."

When the child does a case and the child's first guess is correct, score 100. When the child is correct on the second guess, score 80. If right on the third try, the score would be 60; on the fourth try, a 40; and on the fifth try, a 20.

Figure out the average and keep a record. You will notice that the average will increase with practice.

As the child's guessing factor improves, start selecting more difficult projects. A project can be made more difficult by giving less information to the child about the case. For instance, don't give the child the name of the person involved. Instead just say, "What is worrying the person that I have a picture of in my mind?" Later you can say, "...the person I am thinking of?"

When the child guesses wrong, never tell the child that he or she is wrong. You want to encourage successes. Note down their response and tell them to try again. Give them a multiple choice case and see if they can guess right on the second, third, or fourth guess.

It is important that you remember this: When the child has eyes closed, never say that he or she is wrong. This lowers the child's self-esteem, expectancy, and other genius factors.

When the child is right, get the child to go over the feeling that was associated with the correct guess.

One businessman, a Silva graduate who had been training his own ESP by practicing cases, thought his intuition had led him astray. He was a president of a large manufacturing plant. They needed another site. After considerable study, a site was approved by his comptroller, marketing director, and personnel director. But he said no. Each asked him why. "Gut feeling" was his only reply, as he did not want to confess he used his Silva techniques. Two months later, the state took over that land for highway straightening. He had saved his company a bundle.

A large East Coast university tested successful businessmen on a random number computer to see how their guessing ability compared with unsuccessful businessmen. The criterion for success was to have doubled the company profits in the past three years.

The successful businessmen did twice as well. But they tired. The more they tired, the lower their scores. Then they changed the procedure. Instead of adding up the "hits" at the end, they told each participant "wrong" or "right" immediately. In this way, they began to recognize the feeling of being right and this reversed the trend. Instead of getting poorer, they got better with practice. That is why it is good to have your child know when he or she is right, and remember the feeling at that time. It reinforces rightness.

Just because the executives in that university tired, do not go easy on your child. They were not going to alpha. The child is. It is energy-expending effort at beta; duck soup at alpha.

Remember these points:

1. The child should be between 7 and 14 years of age.

2. Have the child explain what they have seen in full detail and color with eyes closed.

3. Practice for 15 minutes a night once a week, on Sunday night, for example, for three consecutive weeks.

4. Use only problem cases where people are suffering.

5. Never, never say "wrong" when the child's eyes are closed.

6. Work 10 cases and average out the results to observe the child's development.

7. Reinforce the correct guesses by reviewing them. Also have the child recall the feeling associated with the success.

Exercising the psi factor, which is the ability to guess correctly, is a priority activity.

The second priority is to introduce the child to knowledge of the area of work chosen by you and your mate.

Television programs about the profession or occupation chosen are fine. So are movies. When reading is involved, one of the parents should read out loud, showing the child any photos connected with the newspaper or magazine articles.

This reading aloud should be done in a spontaneous manner rather than as a required duty. "Oh, look at this!" is better than "It's time to...."

It would be ideal if teachers, apprised of the special program for your child, could implement that program with special projects.

Hopefully in the near future, educators will be more aware of the importance of the right brain and will be more motivated to participate in the making of a genius.

Even if they are not, you and your mate should have a talk with your child's teachers, one at a time, explaining the Silva Method and its advantages, and outlining steps you are taking to exploit those advantages for your child—all with the purpose of lighting a fire under the teachers at best, or flushing out the skeptics at worst.

Should the skeptics outnumber the others, you might want to investigate other nearby schools if the transfer privilege exists in your area.

Our present educational system does not recognize the learning potential of a human being. In emerging countries, where children are required to pitch in and help parents even as toddlers, they show remarkable ability to carry out simple tasks in a day or two of observation. Reeds are gathered, piled, and bundled by a 3-year-old. Goats are milked by a 4-year-old. A 2-year-old collects eggs in a henhouse.

In many European countries, preschool children help in the markets, bagging merchandise and making change. Others offer trinkets to tourists or work in the fields.

I was 4 years old when my father died in a terrorist act during the Mexican Revolution. My mother remarried and moved to another city in Texas, and I lived with my grandmother.

I began wondering about life at that early age. I was now without both parents. My uncle Manuel lived with my grandmother. He worked in a nearby steam laundry and his pay was barely enough to sustain us. Two blocks away was another building occupied by a British smelting company. Uncle Manuel made me a shoe shine box. I began to make extra money for our household by shining shoes in front of the laundry and smelting company.

It was fun. I enjoyed the people. I decided I could do more and I began selling newspapers. If I didn't shine somebody's shoes, I sold them a newspaper. Uncle Manuel helped me prepare separate lists. On one were the names, addresses, and office numbers of those who wanted shoe shines and when. On the other, those who wanted daily newspapers. On a third, those who wanted both. These lists helped me be in the right place at the right time, giving my customers better service from me. Looking back, I consider this experience a lot better than knowledge or first grade.

Looking back, I also see that I was using my left brain to keep records and supplies, and my right brain to come up with imaginative ideas to better serve my customers. I'm not saying I was a genius, but what I was doing was giving me a better real-life education than a classroom.

Soon I was earning a dollar a day, then two dollars a day. This was now more than Uncle Manuel was making in the laundry. Because the family was in such a financial struggle, it was decided that I would continue working rather than start school.

I began a third activity: Grocery stores put out circulars on Sundays to advertise the next week's prices. They paid me to hand these out. One day I was imagining what the smelting company's offices looked like; who cleaned them. Did each person take care of their own? Just then, the general manager stopped by for a shoe shine. I asked him, "Sir, would you like me to clean your office at the end of the day?"

"How much do you want?" he asked.

I had not done my homework. "Whatever you want to pay me," I replied.

"I'll try you out for a week," he replied.

I arrived that afternoon at closing time. He was getting ready to leave.

"Sweep, dust, wash the windows, and oil the furniture," he brusquely ordered, and he left.

I decided to also empty the pencil sharpeners, install paper in the toilet, and mop the floors. Then I took all the trash and placed it outside for the trash collectors. One day I found a five dollar bill on the floor. Another day I found a watch on the desk. I knew intuitively I was being tested and each time I put the item in a drawer and the next day I told the manager what I had found and where I had put them.

I was not only hired on a regular basis by the manager, but was given other offices to clean at so much per office. Now I was selling newspapers and shining shoes weekdays, distributing circulars on Sundays, and cleaning offices at night.

What was I missing out on at school? One and one make two, while I was counting my profits for the day. C-A-T spells cat, while I was calling out the newspaper headline of the day. Coloring with crayons, while I was polishing furniture and shining shoes.

I'm sure my 6- and 7-year-old education in the outside world can be topped by many other children forced by economic circumstances to educate themselves. The point is: Your genius-in-the-making should not be spared any opportunity that arises for exposure to expanded experiences, for investigating unknown places, for trying out new skills, and for imaginative new games, toys, and entertainment.

My non-instructional education snow-balled: By 12 I was driving my uncle's Ford Model T and chauffeuring a wealthy lady around town to collect her rents. I was cutting lawns and doing odd jobs. I was driving 150 miles to San Antonio to buy merchandise at wholesale not available in Laredo to peddle it door-to-door. Soon I hired a crew of youngsters to work for part of the profits.

I asked them what they were learning in school. It did not click with me because I saw no purpose in it. Was it plane geometry? English? History? Whatever. At any rate, the unschooled boy was the boss, and the school boys were his workers. Symbolic.

I don't intend to demean the educational system. However, going to school and entering the classroom each day should involve, like life, a new adventure. Children have a natural curiosity about nature, people, the out-of-doors, business, manufacturing, farming, and other life activities. Instead of exploiting this, the rote of learning suppresses it.

Children are expected to learn about real life in an artificial environment. No tree, but a picture of a tree. No fish, just a picture of a fish. No survival problem, just a blackboard problem. What motivation can there possibly be each day being in the same classroom with the same people, the same scene out the window, the same smells?

Traditional classroom teaching runs 180 degrees counter to the way the brain learns new things. The brain learns new things not by knowing about these new things, but by directly experiencing new things. Students need to become the things they are studying.

Your child should not leave school, but you need to add another dimension of education to the classroom education now being received. That dimension can be summed up as real life experiences.

Your budding genius deserves more than the incredible boredom and drudgery of one room. School field trips provide occasional opportunities for "hands on" education, but they are far too infrequent. How about adding some home "field trips." Where? Well, perhaps out to where some new home is being built, or to where dad or mom works, or to the airport.

Give it to your child as a case or problem so solve—what kind of a field trip would you benefit most from? Remind the child of the career that lies ahead. Perhaps there is a way to observe a person in that position doing the job. A genius who will be a doctor may benefit by touring a hospital. An investment counselor-to-be may enjoy watching the stock market in action or a local brokerage. A budding lawyer may enjoy being a courtroom spectator.

It's all so simple once you remember that we all were born to be geniuses, and we would continue to be geniuses if we did not mature. Our parents interfere with dismal evaluations of us. "Wet your bed once more and I'll rub your face in it." "You're grounded!" "No television for one week." "I'm stopping your allowance." "You're a clumsy brat!" "Don't tell me that baloney." "Go to bed."

This is all demeaning to a child. It gives the child feelings of guilt for not having done better or differently. It puts down the child.

A genius needs to be put up. A genius thrives on recognition of accomplishment, of appreciation of ability and efforts, and reinforcement of special skills and expertise.

Remember, earlier in this chapter I repeated several times that parents should never say "wrong" in a guessing game while the child has his or her eyes closed. Well, the same holds true for putting down the child, eyes closed or open. Boost the child's self-esteem rather than cloud it. That self-esteem is saying to the brain neurons, "You're tops." So the brain neurons behave "tops."

It would be disastrous to a genius-in-the making to provide input that decreases expectations of wondrous accomplishments. That high expectation is the backbone of a genius-to-be. You don't have to lie. Just don't comment on shortcomings, and use words that are less judgmental. There is always a way of avoiding the negative and emphasizing the positive.

Section V: Prosperity and Abundance

Chapter 15
Ensuring That All Your Needs Are Met

We all need money in order to acquire life's material necessities. "Money is the fuel that keeps the machinery going," my father said. "If you want to do great things, you must have a lot of money to do it with. If you have little things to do in life, you don't need too much money to do whatever that is."

The bigger your plans are, he said, the more money you need. By big plans he meant, "How many people will benefit from what you do."

Some people may think that the term "business ethics" is an oxymoron. But when you understand the spiritual principles that higher intelligence respects, then it makes sense.

Think of it on a personal level. Who would you rather do business with, a person who tries to get as much as possible for himself and give as little as possible in return, or a person who strives hard to give you those three desirable ingredients: quality, price, and service? Wouldn't you prefer to do business with the person who gives you a good quality item at a reasonable price and provides excellent customer service even after the transaction is complete?

My father's formula for prosperity and abundance was simple: "If you need more money in order to implement your plans, then go to your level and think about ways that you can provide better products or better service, and keep in mind what your needs are...plus a little bit more." Whenever we needed more money for the company, he would go teach more classes, or develop a new product to help people.

We prosper in business by helping others to also prosper. He put it this way: "We don't want to gain at somebody else's loss; we want to gain while helping the other person to also gain."

Good citizenship is good business. Apple Computer won some new fans when they fixed a computer for free and shipped it back overnight after they found out that the person, a friend of mine, has multiple sclerosis and is confined to his home. Now there's a good company. That was back in 2004, and look at their success they have had since then, with the iPod and other products.

United Parcel Service (UPS) is another good company, and employees such as Joe Lopez are one of the reasons why. He went out of his way to do something nice one Christmas eve, and that simple act of kindness had a profound effect. My coauthor Ed Bernd Jr. told me about it later.

> After going through more than 50 Christmases, I had finally decided to give up on Christmas. They never lived up to their promise, they always left me disappointed. So I'd decided I was not going to celebrate Christmas ever again.

Ed's mother had died just a few days before.

> It didn't make me sad. I hadn't had much contact with her for several years. But it did bring back memories of the beatings, and how she was always doing everything she could to help everybody else, but not her own family.
>
> Even in death she was still stirring up trouble. She had stipulated that her body be donated to a medical school, but had done it in a way that would start arguments among family members. My youngest sister tipped me off to what was happening, and the two of us just opted out of everything. We didn't want anything, and didn't want to get caught up in the drama.

Ed attended the office Christmas party, which started at noon on Christmas eve. A couple of hours later, after the employee gift exchange, and after my father had given gifts to everybody, Ed walked home to his apartment two blocks away.

> As I sat there thinking about things, there was a knock at the door. It was Joe Lopez with a package for me.
>
> That surprised me, because the package was addressed to the office, and Joe had never delivered a package to my home before.
>
> Joe always came by our office late in the day, just before closing, to make it easier for us to ship all of the orders that came in that day, and thus help as many people as possible. So when he got to the office on that Christmas eve, it was already closed.

I asked him how he knew where to bring the package, and he re-minded me that he had seen me walking back and forth. We'd wave to each other. And evidently, he must have seen which one of the 96 apartments I lived in when he was making a delivery to someone in the complex.

I don't know how to explain how much that meant to me, Ed contin-ued. Here I was, telling myself that I was never going to celebrate another Christmas ever again because it never lived up to its expectations, and Joe Lopez took the trouble to make an extra stop, late in the day on Christmas eve, to drive over to the apartment complex, carry the package upstairs and knock on a door where he'd caught a glimpse of me one time—we don't have names on the doors, or even on the mailboxes—and he didn't know whether I was home, or out doing some last minute Christmas shopping.

The package was from my youngest sister. We've always had a special relationship, and it meant a lot to me to get a gift from her.

It also meant a lot to me that Joe Lopez took the extra effort, and spent a few minutes of his time when he could have waited and delivered the package to the office the day after Christmas, and could have gone home to his family a few minutes earlier that Christmas eve.

The story doesn't end there. Here is the best part:

That night, I was thinking about a friend of mine, the closest friend I've had in many years. We were like brothers, we could both anticipate what the other was going to do or say. We had such similar goals and ideas that we started a business together.

One of the similarities was that we both came from very dysfunctional backgrounds. His mother had died when he was 6 years old, and when his father remarried, he placed him in an orphanage. His childhood had been even worse than mine.

My friend and I found it difficult to work together. Our insecurities and frustrations created friction between us, and earlier that same year we had dissolved the business. We pretty much dissolved our friendship too. Neither of us wanted to hurt the other one, but that's what we had been doing, so we had little contact with one another.

We had both read John Bradshaw's books and watched his videos about "healing the wounded child within." We had a good understanding of the problem, but Bradshaw hadn't offered any solutions that worked for us. I tried beating up a pillow one night, but it didn't do a thing for me. We knew the answer would have to come from within, from deep levels of mind. From a place where the "wounded child within" resides.

When I went to bed on that Christmas eve, I was thinking about my friend, and trying—as I had done so many times before—to figure out what had gone wrong, what I could have done differently, what I could do now to make him feel better and to exorcize some of those demons that both of us are so familiar with. I was at a very deep level as I did this, at the alpha brain wave level where we have access to more information, "ventilate impediments" as Jose Silva's brother Juan put it.

Looking back, I'm pretty sure that if Joe Lopez had not gone to the trouble of bringing me the present from my sister, I would have been thinking about how disappointing Christmas was yet again, instead of searching for some kind of help for my friend.

Specifically, I was thinking about how his mother's death when he was so young left him feeling abandoned and, as young children do, wondering if she left him because she didn't love him. Did it leave him feeling unloved, unwanted, unlovable? He is a wonderful person, but did he know it? Did the "wounded child" inside of him know it?

Suddenly "it came to me" that my mother had experienced the same thing as my friend. Her mother died when she was very young, and her father, whose job required constant travel, put her in a boarding house, and that's where she grew up.

Just like my friend, my mother was raised by strangers. So she must have felt the same way: abandoned, unloved, unwanted, unlovable. No wonder she treated us so badly, and tried so hard to prove to everyone else that she was a good person.

If she felt that she was unloved, unwanted, unlovable, then anybody associated with her—the man who married her, and even her own children—must have something terribly wrong with them. No wonder she treated her children so badly. It wasn't our fault, it wasn't about us. She was lashing out at herself.

It was quite a revelation, another piece of information for the adult Ed to analyze. And it was more than that. It was something that the wounded child Edward could accept. It is very difficult to fool children. They know whether or not people are being honest with them. If you are trying to get them to do something because it will benefit *you*, they know...and they don't trust you.

But this time, I was not seeking anything for myself. I had received two wonderful gifts a few hours earlier—the present from my sister, and Joe's thoughtfulness in bringing it to me. I wasn't thinking the thoughts that I was thinking in order to convince the wounded child inside of *me* that he was okay, that he was a wonderful kid and a perfect person. I wasn't trying to relieve my own pain.

So the child within me realized that if I had no ulterior motive, then it must be true.

Now I didn't realize any of that at the time. In fact, when I woke up the next morning, I didn't even recall any of it. In fact, I still had the idea that I was not going to celebrate Christmas ever again.

But something strange was going on. Christmas carols were playing on the radio and they sounded wonderful; they were bringing me more joy and happiness than ever before. When the song about Good King Wenceslas came on, I knew for certain that something was up. I always thought that was the dumbest song ever written. What the heck is "the feast of Eden" anyway?

The song sounded great. I was loving it. What in the world was wrong? Something had changed, something was happening. I was pacing the floor, restless. Why?

Then I remembered that before I went to sleep, I had been thinking of something interesting. I had no idea what it was. I remembered that I had been at a very very deep level, as deep as I have ever been.

So I sat down, entered my level, and picked up the first thing that I could recall from the night before. I remembered that I had been thinking about my friend, how he must have felt when his mother died, and then I remembered how I had recognized that the same thing had happened to my mother.

It all came back to me. And it made sense. It made sense both to adult Ed and to the child Edward, who was no longer such a wounded child.

Had there really been a breakthrough? Or was this just another intellectual exercise? I'd had insights before. Was this one different? It sure felt different. The real test—the test for "reality"—would come in my ability to perform better in the future than I had in the past.

And I sure did. For starters, people who had tended to dismiss my ideas in the past suddenly seemed eager to hear what I had to say. Wow, what a wonderful new experience.

In addition to giving me a sense of peace and confidence and self-esteem I'd only heard about but had never experienced before, there was also a major impact on my work.

When I wrote the *Think and Grow Fit* book with Mr. Silva the next year, I was much more relaxed, and it showed. Many people told me that it was the best writing I had ever done, much better than the previous book, *Sales Power*, which was very successful and was translated into more than a dozen other languages.

My recordings changed too. In the past I had read scripts and tried hard to sound natural. Now I began working from notes instead of scripts, being more spontaneous, and speaking from the heart. Something inside me had changed, and I no longer had a fear of revealing myself. Once again, people commented on the improvement.

More and more people were benefiting from what had happened. And it all started when Joe Lopez took the time to track me down and deliver a package instead of hurrying up to finish and rush home like many people were doing on Christmas eve.

So the next time you are tempted to pass up an opportunity to do something nice for somebody, remember this: It might not make a bit of difference. Then again, you might be missing a chance to have a positive impact on a lot of lives and improve conditions on the planet, the way Joe Lopez did.

And how does Ed feel about Christmas now?

"It reminds me of how wonderful people can be, and that makes me feel very good."

PROPER PROGRAMMING

Now that you understand the spiritual principles underlying good business practices, and you know how to use the MentalVideo to help you find out what higher intelligence wants you to do, let's take a look at the best way to program to obtain the resources that you need, and to carry out your assignment.

Some people have the wrong idea about how to program to get things, so let's set the record straight right now.

Rather than thinking about what you want and how you will feel when you get something or achieve something, it is far better to think about how the success will correct problems, how it will relieve suffering, how it will help someone to achieve his or her purpose in life, and how it will make the world a better place to live.

If you need a new car (not *want*, but *need*), then don't think about how you will feel when you get it, how proud you will be of yourself. Instead, think about the problem you will solve by having the new car: your family will be safer, you will get to places on time, you will be able to help other people. Remember, the more people who will benefit, the easier it will be to achieve your goal.

My father used to say that "We were not sent here on a 70 year vacation. We were sent here with a job to do, and that job is to correct problems and to make the world a better place to live, to finish the creation and convert the world into a paradise.

"We suffer because of ignorance," he said. "If we know what we are supposed to do and how to do it, then we will not suffer. We can create a paradise. That's our job, that is why we were sent here," he believed. And his research supported that, because when he used that attitude—and when others of us have that attitude—we accomplish things and improve conditions.

It is not about us and what we want and how we feel. We can have everything we need to do our jobs, plus more, provided that we are actually doing our jobs, which is what higher intelligence sent us here to do, and that is to correct problems, relieve suffering, and make the world a better place to live.

So focus on doing that, not on yourself, and you will get much better results.

He included a line at the very end of the conditioning cycles, the most powerful place in the conditioning cycle, that we should "strive to take part in constructive and creative activities to make this world a better place to live, so that when we move on we shall have left behind a better world for those who follow."

"As I was explaining that in class one weekend," Ed Bernd recalled, "it occurred to me just how special that statement is. Does it make sense? If we are worried about getting things for ourselves, why would we comply with that statement—to do things that will benefit people long after we are gone, when there is no way that we could possibly gain anything, no way that those people who come along later could compensate us for the benefits they receive from our work?

"When I saw Mr. Silva in the office on Monday," Ed continued "I mentioned it to him. 'That's a statement of unselfishness, isn't it?' I asked. He didn't answer directly. His eyes lit up and he looked at me and said, 'If it weren't for that attitude, we wouldn't have the Silva Method today.'"

Not everyone wants to accept these ideas, and they certainly have the right to accept or reject anything they choose. But if you look around, you can find plenty of evidence to support this. Because my father had the correct attitude, millions of people around the world have benefitted from his research.

This is from a transcript from a recording of my father during a seminar he called the Metaphysical Laws of Success Course conducted here in Laredo in 1996:

The other side will only help me when I am asking for something that is needed to improve conditions on planet earth.

Like we said, they are not going to help me if I want another million dollars when I already have a million dollars, when I want a Rolls Royce when I have a Rolls Royce already. That I want a girlfriend when I already have a wife. Some people ask for something like this.

They are not going to help you. You are on your own. If you make a mistake, you are going to suffer for it, you are on your own. You don't get help from the other side.

You only get help from the other side when your intentions are that whatever you are doing is to help improve conditions on the planet for more than yourself, not just yourself. Then you ask for help, and you are going to get it immediately.

Once you understand this, then you are on the right track.

It is about what your intentions are. You are walking down the street tomorrow and see a board with a nail sticking out. Ninety-nine percent of the people walking by just kick it aside, saying, "Somebody's going to get hurt with that. Let them take care of it, what the heck do I care about it."

Yes, you should care. You should pick it up, get the nail out of the way before somebody gets hurt.

Once you are aware of this, you should pick it up and put it aside before somebody gets hurt. This is how we are supposed to be functioning on this planet, and we're not. We don't care for one another.

This "love one another" means "help one another." That's what it meant. You help me and I'll help you. Everybody helps each other, that would be great.

We have a saying: At alpha we should pray *for* one another. At beta we prey *on* one another.

We want to gain by helping others gain, not gain at somebody else's loss.

If you only consider Me, you have to do it on your own. If it is for Us, then you get help, if whatever you do is going to help more than you.

The more you are going to help, the more help you get for it.

We always say, "Don't ever ask for more than what you need, but do ask for no less than what you need."

So what your needs will be depends on how big your plans are. That's what your needs will be.

He went on to explain that "how big your plans are" means "how many people will benefit." The more people who benefit, the better.

RECOGNIZING AND ACCEPTING OUR GUIDANCE

It is not always easy to accept the guidance we get. I recall one time when one of our most productive instructors was not adhering to our policies. We had to tell him that if he didn't conform to the policies the same as everybody else is required to, we would have to terminate his contract. We didn't want to do that, because we would have lost a great deal of income, and he knew it.

We used the MentalVideo, hoping that higher intelligence would help us to get the message across to the instructor. Instead, higher intelligence had a message for us. The very next day, after using the MentalVideo, we got class reports—and nice royalty checks—from two instructors who usually didn't have very large classes. We took this as an indication from higher intelligence that we would still have plenty of business and income even if the one very productive instructor decided to quit. So we stuck to our guns, we let the instructor know that we were very serious, and the end result was that he agreed to follow all of our policies in the future.

The indications that we get from higher intelligence are not always big and spectacular. They are often relatively normal things, and if you are not looking for them, you might never know that you are receiving help from your "invisible means of support," higher intelligence. Fortunately, we were looking for indications of how to proceed, and we realized that the two unexpected class reports were bringing us a message. And it didn't stop there. Later an old friend called to say he was sending us a $10,000 donation, and before the day was over we got another excellent class report we didn't expect.

In the next chapter we'll look at how people are using ESP to help them in business and in life.

Chapter 16
ESP in Business

Sometimes the indications are quick and obvious; sometimes they take a little longer. The following are examples of indications in business.

Dolores, our friend who works in the high-tech industry in the northwestern U.S., sent us this experience back in February of 2005:

> Well, I think all my grumbling to higher intelligence about the way things are going in my job at the moment (frenzied and stressful for the time-being) may have worked.
>
> This morning my boss walked into my office and handed me an envelope while telling me how much he really appreciates all the effort I've been putting into my work since coming on. Inside the envelope was quite a generous bonus. (Hmmmm, I wonder if he knows I goof off and take those "mini-vacations" on the job that you told me about?) He told me that once we get through the bottleneck we are currently working to get through, things should be back to normal again.
>
> Anyway, in my grumblings to HI [higher intelligence] I certainly didn't specifically ask for this bonus, only an indication of some sort that I either should or should not continue on with this company. What do you think? Was this an indication?

Since she asked, we answered. Here is the analysis that we sent to her:

> When he came and complimented you and assured you that things will settle down soon and he told you how much he appreciated you, that was a good indication. I always like to consider proximity to the MentalVideo. So you asked, and he came and told you. It meets all the

criteria: Anybody could have seen what happened; it was objective, in the physical dimension.

But you know the old sayings: Talk is cheap. By their acts ye shall know them.

So he literally put his money where his mouth was!

Let's face it, somebody might want to compliment (flatter) you and say reassuring things just to get you to keep working through the current bottleneck. And then, who knows what might happen.

So I'd say the cash was a second indication; one that not only confirms the first, but does it in a way that leaves no doubt. They are not likely to invest money in somebody who might be departing the premises anytime soon.

So I think it's a pretty "kewl" experience and example of how this stuff can work.

A few months later Dolores encountered more challenges, as often happens in the high-tech industry. After thinking about programming for what *she* wanted, she decided to ask for help from higher intelligence for both herself and for her husband, who had applied for a great job on the other side of the state.

I don't want to meddle at this point. I will leave this up to HI and tutors and step aside from the characters. I learned my lesson because my programming got me into a job (current one) that I am not entirely happy with. It seemed perfect when I started, exactly what I wanted, but is certainly less than perfect several months later.

We answered:

You can trust the formula. Review the MentalVideo formula: You create a video of how *you* think things should go, and then look for indications of how to proceed.

Our attitude has always been: *This is what I think, and I'm going to keep working on it unless you tell me otherwise. So if you want me to stop, or to do something different, please let me know.*

They always let us know!

About a week later, Dolores got the word about the layoffs. Here is what she wrote to us:

My boss called me into his office yesterday morning, told me to close the door. Said there is a layoff about to occur, said the whole company is downsizing to a leaner, meaner more focused team, told me he was going to release me.

He then smiled and went on to say there is another group in the company who really wants me and he, and others who are pulling for me, got me a position with them. What that group does is more in alignment with what he originally brought me on to do for him (actually an even better fit) before things were reorganized and my duties changed to what I currently don't like doing. Anyway, all this while I have been in daily communication with my tutors, giving them feedback on what has been going on. I think they have been listening…as usual.

I also did a MentalVideo on Wednesday evening, asking for some guidance/indication with regard to my husband interviewing for a job on the other side of the State, which would require a really big move for us. I asked for some clear indication because we haven't heard anything yet about a decision (in government these decisions take time, decision by committee, etc.). I'd like to know if I should just quit right now and take a chance because I don't like my job? Then this all happened at work on Friday. What do you think? Indication?!

What's more, my boss told me that the guy they just hired to help me out is going to be laid off. He doesn't know it yet. *And* what my manager doesn't know is that the guy wants to be laid off, has been wanting it for some time, he told me this in confidence about a week ago. He has been with the company for awhile, transferred in from another department. His home is elsewhere, in another state. Had he not come to work with me this would not have happened. Funny how all these things just "sort of" come together. That also explains why even though he and I were apples and oranges, as far as our work backgrounds go, we were brought together to work. Makes you realize there is often a big plan at work and that somehow we are all interconnected. And now I realize that big plan has been working out for a long time.

And now for the happy ending to this story that you have been waiting for:

I meant to tell you that since John got turned down for that job on the other side of the state, he has been getting a flood of clients coming to *him* for a record number of projects. Our company is doing really well this year. Remember I said I knew it was for the better that he didn't get that job? I wasn't that fired up about moving.

The work I am doing now is 1,000% better than what I was doing with the client I recently left. The pay is truly amazing, hard to believe I am getting paid so much for doing so little, and it is easy work. Getting paid while waiting around for something to do if needed. I am not complaining. It's giving me a lot more time to study, work on my research for my dissertation. I'm home doing that today. Remember how I said I needed to program for more time and to get off that previous project as gracefully as possible? That's exactly what happened. I really like the people on this new project. Very upbeat and friendly.

That last project I was on is in trouble. You know that guy that hired me on with really enticing work, and then switched my project on me to one I hated and wasn't suited for—and that was all screwed-up such that the previous guy just up and left it? Then I got that bonus to "make things better"? I saw him last week and asked how it was going. He said, "I don't know," with a slight grimace. Nice guy, but so glad I'm not working for them anymore.

Higher intelligence works in such wonderful ways.

We couldn't agree more.

How to Help a Really Bad Boss

Su Irons, a Silva graduate in New Zealand, improved a bad situation by helping her bad boss find another job. Here is how she did it:

Work got to be extremely depressing—well, not work exactly, the general manager [GM] to be precise. A true blue real and utter you-know-what!

That GM terrorized a good portion of the staff for just over three and a half years. He specialized in singling someone out and picking on them consistently for months on end. He would also find fault with whatever one did.

For the past 12 months, my confidence having been zapped so much I didn't have the energy to go find another job, I've been programming that he would get a job offer he couldn't possibly refuse, and in his place we'd have a replacement who would be at the best possible person to manage the Auckland SPCA.

I've been practising Silva long enough not to be stunned by results. But boy was I *stunned*, when on 23 November we were all summoned by the GM into the boardroom for a short meeting—where he announced his resignation final day 24 Dec. Apparently, he had been "tapped on the shoulder" by another charity.

The GM had sent an e-mail around on the Wednesday ordering staff to be in the boardroom at noon next day for a short meeting. My assistant, Virginia, groaned and said, "Whatever have we all done wrong now?" I chirped up and flippantly said, "Well, y'know, I guess he's had an offer he simply can't refuse and he's going to tell us he's resigned." I got a very rude sound back from Virginia.

You can imagine her face next day at the meeting. When we got back to the office she said I must've known, till I reminded her that I was the very last person the GM would let know what was going on. She had to agree with that—but she's remained very impressed with my "lucky guess." Come to that, so am I.

That night when I went to bed I thanked the Universe, Silva-wise, for helping us all out. And I asked if it wasn't too much trouble it would be greatly appreciated by the staff if "they" could arrange for the GM's replacement to be the best possible person for the job.

At the GM's official farewell on Thursday 23 December, the board president announced the new GM—who just happens to be a board member, and is a really nice, approachable person whom just about everybody likes, and who has been involved with SPCA for years. She's been working in Spain for the past five months or so, but is chucking that in to move back here for the GM position, which I know will be paying far less than her present job. So, really dedicated too. Fantastic news. It looks like next year will make up for the past two and a half years from hell.

I'm still blown away by the response to my request to higher intelligence, as I didn't even think in my wildest imagination that Jane would be the replacement.

I still find it really difficult to put my faith in the Universe. Hopefully, they up there are helping me do this. I must be very frustrating for them!

Twice in a month, Silva has completely knocked my socks off. I'm still pinching myself that it's actually all fallen into place and I'm not dreaming.

BUYING AND SELLING

A Silva graduate named Penny Atwell is a real estate broker in Maine. After many years, she and her husband decided to sell their old farmhouse and a beach house and move to South Carolina. Even though she has had a lot of successes in the past, she was surprised by how powerful the MentalVideo Technique is.

So timely your suggestions for selling my properties. There's that Silva thing at work again popping up just when I needed a boost!

We are sitting tonight with an offer on one of the properties, the lake house. We got it yesterday, countered to it last night and today got another counter from the buyer, still below what we decided to take. We have written up a proposal with a final counter but we were really unsure as to whether we really want to give it to them.

Then something made me decide to wait till tomorrow to decide if we should relay it to the other broker. And surprise, surprise, there you were with your e-mail and the MentalVideo suggestion. Guess what I'll be doing tonight! Definitely need help deciding if we should just wait these people out and see how badly they want it or wait for the buyer who will pay us what we want.

She wrote later and said there had been some last-minute details to work out, and that things eventually worked out just fine in ways she hadn't anticipated:

It's Penny from Maine and I just thought I'd tell you that my second house just sold!!! Way before we ever thought it would!! I'm still in a state of shock at how quickly it happened and what fantastic buyers we got for my beloved farmhouse. I couldn't have picked more understanding, empathetic buyers if I'd tried. Between Silva and St. Joseph's statue, I had a powerful team on my side. The house has only been listed two weeks!!

And the lake house is almost ready to close too. So I guess I'll be moving to South Carolina much faster that I ever thought would happen. I really am still shell shocked and aside from bursting into tears at the drop of a hat when I think about leaving this wonderful old home, I am happy that I'm spared the agony of having to show it to unappreciative people.

I do feel someone was watching over this old house to make sure its new owners were worthy. These people even brought our dog Bear a gift today when they came back to chat with us!! How can you not like people like that? When one is about 165 years old, as this house is, it needs a caretaker who will know what it needs to keep going. And I believe with Silva help and St. Joseph's intervention, we have found that perfect caretaker to follow us.

And the kicker is how we found them. Their broker never even pulled up our house for them to consider, because we were out of the price range they had specified. But the broker asked for a showing at a house I have listed across the road for less money. I just suddenly felt that I should mention our house because they'd be right here, even though it was more than they said they'd spend. She agreed to bring them to our house, and here we are. Did I have help from somewhere? You won't convince me otherwise!

I truly believe that we can help make things happen as long as we *desire* them, *believe* it will happen, and *expect* the results we want. I have been so lucky to have gotten so much good from this that I feel bad when I lapse and just trust to happenstance. And I know better, but I don't always remember to ask for help. Maybe the graduate support group Website will help others like me, semi-occasional lapsed Silva grads remember the gift they have learned to use. So keep working on it, use anything of mine you wish to use if you think it good enough to help someone else, and I'll be waiting to be inspired by others successes too.

Even though they had reached an agreement for the sale of the old farmhouse, there was still more to do, and Penny continued to program.

Just thought I'd update you with our continuing Silva success with my two houses. Not without some last minute glitches, last minute huddles with our attorney and lots of last minute tension, our lake house finally closed last Friday. One down, one to go.

And thanks to some major programming the dreaded building inspection on my old farmhouse went fine and even though there were things the inspector pointed out, our wonderful buyers asked us to fix *nothing*!!! They made *no* comment on the inspection at all, just accepted it. We are grateful beyond belief. Steve was so appreciative that he's leaving them our generator as a thank you. You don't find many buyers like that, I can assure you, and I continue to know that I had help from somewhere in finding and keeping them. And so we wind ever closer to our moving date...somewhere in the third week of August.

INTERACTING WITH OTHER PEOPLE

A Silva graduate in Japan, Tomoki Takahashi, was programming to find a new home for himself and his wife when he first wrote to us. Then he also started using the MentalVideo Technique. Here is what happened:

I was using the Subjective Communication Technique first. We made a list of our ideal flat and the quality of landlord or landlady, and made our own subjective communication recording.

The recording included the specific things that we wanted in our new flat, including an honest, friendly, and responsible landlord or landlady.

After playing the subjective communication recording twice or so, we started looking for a flat in the same village where my friend had recently moved in, because we found the location of his flat is convenient and it is in a quiet environment. We went back a couple of times, but couldn't find any *Vacancy* signs at all. We were a little disappointed and we discussed that we might as well focus on a different town or village, not near the village where my friend lives.

A week later, my wife and I went back to the village where my friend lives, because I had an intuition that we should go back to the area again. We had listened to the Subjective Communication recording and the MentalVideo recording consecutively for three nights.

We walked the same route as the previous times, hoping that there would be some vacancies. We found a sign on a shabby building and phoned the real estate agency. However, the rent was more expensive than we had expected. We gave up and continued walking towards the center of the town. We took a shortcut and we seemed to have gotten lost. Then we turned around, we found a newly built block of flats on our left. There was a vacancy sign on the top of the building, but the phone number was for a real estate agency that had told us there were no vacancies there.

While we were checking the building from outside, we heard men talking and one of them came out. My wife rushed to him and asked him the details about the flat. To our surprise, there were five vacant flats there. In addition to that, he was the owner of the building and showed us all the flats. The rent and the conditions seem to match our needs. Both my wife and I loved it. As soon as we went out from the building, I went to the level to scan the owner to check if he is a responsible person and we knew he was a proper person, so we moved a month earlier that we had planned.

This is how we found our new home.

Thank you very much again for your assistance. My wife and I are very happy about the new flat. Our next goal is to immigrate to the USA earlier. We have already applied for our green cards to the United States, but it may take another four to five years, so we want to get them faster. As I mentioned before, we haven't had the telephone and Internet lines installed yet. It might take another one month, so in case you need to contact me about the story in case you want to put my story in your new book and have difficulty understanding what I wrote, you can phone at any time.

GUIDED TO A NEW JOB

A lady who lives in the New Jersey area obtained the Silva UltraMind ESP System home study course and learned some new tools for helping other people. Better still, she is showing other people how to use these tools to help themselves.

Here are two stories from her:

As you say, "This stuff works good." If you want some anecdotal data, here is some: A friend of my daughter's came to the door last Sunday to deliver a package. We started talking and he told me he had just resigned from a dead-end job. His prospects were not too good. He had had a terrible childhood, no education, minimal jobs since, and health problems.

I asked him to visualize his ideal job through the 3-Scenes Technique, just before going to bed. He came the next morning to listen to the first CD, then Tuesday for the second one, with an announcement: An acquaintance of his sister's had come in person to his house on Monday with an offer of a job that will permit him to make enough money that he can go back to community college, and the time to do it! Talk about fast!

And a second story: My 7-year-old hyperactive grandson could not play a piano or violin piece without making lots of errors. I tried to make him listen to the Long Relaxation Exercise, but keeping his eyes closed was an impossibility. I tried the Short Relax without much success either.

He would scream: "That alpha stuff doesn't work, I want to stay angry," and so on. I suggested then that he go in his mind where he sees colors, that it would be alpha, and then play his music piece before doing it on the instrument.

Last night, we went to his house, and his mother suggested he play. A very different sound was heard: He was poised, deliberate, and accurate. Of course, we praised him sky high.

I asked him for the secret that brought out such change. His response: "Alpha." Imagine the goose bumps.

So I'm very grateful for all these blessings coming out so fast and my heartfelt thanks to Jose Silva and your keeping up his mission. Now, I also have more confidence in helping to heal this planet, one person at a time. God bless you.

HELP OTHERS AND WE HELP OURSELVES

Klemen Mihelic is a new Silva UltraMind ESP System instructor in Slovenia, and he has been practicing the MentalVideo Technique so he can teach others how to use it. He started by using it to resolve a problem he encountered on the construction of a new house.

"We had problems with our seller/investor who did not build the house as we both agree at the beginning," Klemen explained. "There were too many mistakes."

First he tried to correct the problem on his own by entering his level and picturing all of the mistakes corrected with the 3-Scenes Technique, and the seller giving him some money to compensate him for the deficiencies.

"As I look back now," he said, "I realize that I really wanted too much money."

He first realized this after programming with the MentalVideo to obtain some guidance from higher intelligence. Armed with this new information, and remembering the Laws of Programming and how the solution should be the best thing for everybody concerned, he went to level again to see what ideas would come to him to help resolve the matter.

I went to level and simply tried to solve the problem with the seller. I told him, mentally, about mistakes and delays, and at my level he told a me few things that I had not considered. That is why I lower my requests to him. At my level we both agreed with some corrections on the building, and we also agreed with a discount of $15,500.

What happened the next day when I meet the guy was amazing. He offered to correct exactly what I had programmed to be corrected, and he also offered me a discount of exactly $15,500. I was speechless!

Following that, he had another very big success that has turned out to be very beneficial to him, although that was not his original intent. He was simply trying to help a friend who had made a mistake and given up a good job for a job that turned out to be a very bad job; not what he had been promised.

When my friend told me his sad story, I started asking other friends for help. My "beta" plan was to find him some other job as soon as possible.

When I used the MentalVideo, I reviewed the current situation. My friend was doing dirty work. I pictured him sad and worrying about how to support his family. It was very easy to picture him since I spent that evening with him.

In the solution video, I picture myself asking friends, looking over the Internet, and checking news for some job that would be okay. The final part of the solution video was my friend working with computers in some nice office.

The next day when I was driving an idea came to me. I was thinking about some work I should have done one month ago. We needed to pick up some promotional materials that we had used in promotions in six different places around Slovenia.

First I should have gone and collected the material, but I was busy, so I ask my brother if he could go collect it since he had some free time. But somehow I did not find the time to explain to him what exactly he needed to do.

Then my friend from work asked his brother, but since his brother does not have a car, we did not collect the material.

As you see, there was a simple job to do, but we somehow failed to do it over and over. We talked about that so many times.

And suddenly it came to me that I could hire my friend. As I thought about it, I realized that there was a lot of work we do not like to do ourselves that my friend could do.

When I told my friend about my idea, he told me that he is willing to do that kind of work, and that he actually likes it. I immediately knew that we could hire him.

We will have a lot of work to do at our new building. We also need some help with our graphic art work. I was thinking that he can do some basic work at the beginning and learn how to do more. I called him and he agreed. He quit his dirty job and started to work in my company in two days.

I do not know why I did not think about hiring him at the beginning. All I do know is that solution is best for everybody concerned. We are all very happy about the way we solved the problem.

What I see as very important is: Why did we fail to do the work so many times? As Mr. Silva said, all of those "coincidences" let us know that higher intelligence was guiding us to a solution that many people benefited from long before we even knew about the problem.

DEALING WITH DIFFICULT PEOPLE

Chen Jie sent us this story from China about using mental projection to solve a problem of an account number and password being stolen:

I run an internet office. Around 9 a.m. on November 20, 2006, I came to my office. The working staff on the night shift reported that around 3 a.m., the Internet was down. We tried several times to make it work, but found that my account number and password to log in had been stolen.

I brought my ID to the telecommunications department to apply to change my password. I asked the telecommunications people if I could log in after changing my password. I was told that if the person who stole the password logged out, then I could log in. If he didn't log out, I might have to wait 48 hours and then they would automatically change the IP address, the thief would be cut off, and I could log in.

When I came back to my office, I had new staff to be trained. Four computers could not be used because of the stolen password. So I went into another room and sat quietly and went into the level to adjust this abnormality.

First I used Mental Screen Technique to ask that the person who stole my account number and password be shown on my mental screen. In several seconds, a young man around 20 years old appeared. He had a thin face, short hair, and small eyes. He was typing in front of the computer. Behind him was a bed. His room was not big. I wondered what he was doing, so I went behind him and saw him playing computer games. At this moment, one of his friends knocked at the door and came in. They watched the computer and discussed something happily. It seemed that they discussed the contents of the game.

I began to understand that the thief was stealing my account number and password to log in for his personal purpose. So I decided to adjust this abnormality. I cleared the screen and imagined a telephone line that the thief was using. Then I imagined I held scissors and told the thief that "Because you illegally used my account number and had no right to use it, I am cutting off your telephone line."

Then I thought that if I cut off this telephone line, it would affect the whole internet system and others. We should not cause problems for other people, but should do what is best for everyone concerned.

So I decided to revise my plan and used a better one. I used the 3-Scenes Technique and created a story: The cellular phone was ringing on his table. It was his friend inviting him to lunch. After answering the phone, the thief was happy and logged out, turned off the computer, took his jacket, and went out. I designed the time for lunch was 11:30.

After completing the story and procedure, I exited from the level. I watched the clock, which indicated 10:45.

Then I went on working. During this period, my staff tried to log in but failed.

Suddenly I heard one staff shouting out happily, "I can log in now." I looked at the clock again. It was 11:32.

That evening, I told my colleague about this experience. He was very surprised. Though he didn't quite understand, he reminded me that "our clock was two minutes fast. If you saw 11:32, it should be 11:30. Haha."

YOUR INVISIBLE MEANS OF SUPPORT

Here are a couple more stories about how your Everyday ESP can bring you help from what my father called "your invisible means of support" whenever you need it.

James Petry of Worcestershire, UK, sent us what he referred to as "a small story" in January 2004. He has purchased both the UltraMind ESP System and the UltraMind Remote Viewing and Remote Influencing home study courses from us and was practicing with them.

His Everyday ESP kicked in unexpectedly when he was placing a bid for a book on the eBay online auction. Here is his "small story":

There was a certain book available on eBay. Now this book was by Robert Stone, and I believed it would contain techniques that would help me to extend my use of alpha.

So, I took the time to go to level and asked, for the highest good of all, what should I bid on this book?

After a few seconds, a figure came to mind. I made the bid.

Now, I did win, but there was a gap between the figure I was given and my winning bid.

Imagine my surprise when I was told the shipping charge, and the total combined cost to me was within one dollar of the figure I got at level.

I think this is a nice story as it stands, but there is a corollary.

I later discovered that someone else, with more Silva experience than I have, had also been programming at level to acquire that book.

They were willing to bid far more than I was to win, but circumstances prevented them from reaching a computer in time.

However, within three days of the auction closing, they found another source for this rare book and paid less than I did in the end.

Temple Nash is a natural psychic who is also a certified Silva instructor, and who is always happy to program for anybody who needs help. Don't expect him to solve your problems for you, though; he understands that while we can all help one another, we each have to take an active part in solving our own problems.

Temple works for a security firm, and told us about this Everyday ESP experience that seems to have worked in the background without him being consciously aware of it at the time:

My boss told me to go to a job in Wilmer, Texas, from 6 in the morning until 6 at night. I moaned and groaned. Then he called and told me that he had hired somebody for that job and for me to not go to that one, but to a different one.

But when I got up early the next morning, I went to the original job as originally planned because I had forgotten about the second one. It turned out that the guy who they hired for the job I wound up doing never called in and never showed up, so it came out in the wash.

My boss called me and asked where I worked on Saturday. I told him and he thanked God for it. I did not remember him telling me to not go to the first post until after he called me and we discussed it. Turns out that by doing the wrong thing, I actually did the right thing, without even realizing it.

The guys on the second post handled it amongst themselves; they know what I do and they don't get bent out of shape when things don't go according to plan. Heck, we are used to it. As we used to say in the first security company I worked for, you are full grown, deal with it. Then report it the next work day.

There are so many more stories we could tell you about coincidences that occur after we use the MentalVideo. Like the time our lawyer asked us for some information that we thought was completely unnecessary. We got it for him anyway, and in the process, discovered something we had never realized before that gave us exactly what we needed to solve a very big problem.

Then there is a retiree who was wondering if he was going to have enough money, so he programmed with the MentalVideo and the next day he got a letter in the mail from the Social Security Administration telling him they had made a mistake in the amount of his pension payments for the entire year. They had underpaid him, and would be depositing an additional $224 in his account the next month. "That was very reassuring," he said.

We love to hear stories such as these, and to share them with other Silva graduates, so please tell us about your successes with your Everyday ESP.

Chapter 17
ESP for Executives
by John Mihalasky, EdD

In the last few years it has become increasingly difficult for business and industry to stay competitive. Critics charge that there is too much reliance on short-term thinking and on the fear of taking risks.

With more data being generated by more and more computers, there has been a tendency to slip into a posture of "managing by the numbers." The emphasis has been on the use of rationality and logic in problem-solving and decision-making—operations research, management science, modeling, and the development of computers that "think."

Unfortunately, all this has given us more and more incorrect, invalid, and/or unreliable data, faster, to make decisions whose outcomes have been correct about as many times as when we made decisions by holding a wet finger up to the wind.

It is my contention that this state of affairs is due to the fact that not enough has been done to investigate the application of illogical, nonrational, unconscious thinking. We have spent most of our time on rational, logical, conscious thinking. It is (and has been for a long time) necessary to delve into the use of the unconscious.

The purpose of the material in this chapter is to explore the basis for the use of the unconscious—ESP, if you will—in the problem-solving and decision-making processes.

THE PRECOGNITIVE DECISION-MAKER

The PSI Communications Project at the Newark College of Engineering (now the New Jersey Institute of Technology) researched the phenomenon of precognition and the nature of the precognitive decision-maker in the 1960s and 1970s.

There is now evidence to suggest that the successful "hunch player"—a person who makes decisions based on hunches rather than fact or evidence—may have something more solid going for him or her than the odds of chance.

Experiments indicate that what the texts call illogical (and what managers privately call "lucky") decisions have some scientific—that is, observable, dependable, and explainable—support.

The research project strongly supports the idea that some executives have more precognitive ability than others—that is, they are better able to anticipate the future intuitively rather than logically and thus, when put in positions where strong data support may not always exist, will make better decisions.

Moreover, a valid test has been developed for determining which people do, and which do not, have this ability.

The test consists of asking the participants to guess at a 100-digit number not currently in existence. (The numbers would later be computer-generated using random-number techniques.) Each of the 100 digits can take on any value from zero to nine. A computer generates a specific target for each participant.

As expected, some people guess above the chance level of 10 correct guesses out of the 100 digits, while others guess at, or below, the chance level.

That some people score above chance on this test would, by itself, not prove they have precognitive ability. But the research has revealed some interesting and significant relationships between high scores on this simple guessing game and other kinds of data.

For example, participants are asked to rank their preferences among five metaphors (such as "a motionless ocean," "a dashing horseman," and so forth) that have been adapted from a psychological test.

Based on their choices, the subjects are divided into "dynamic" and "nondynamic" types. Admittedly, this is not a very sophisticated classification. But invariably, those classified as dynamic by this relatively simple means also tend to score above chance in predicting the computer's random numbers.

In tests on 27 different groups, ranging from four members to 100, dynamic people outscored nondynamic people in 22 of the groups. Statistically, the chances of this happening by accident are fewer than five in 1,000. Many other groups were tested after this initial 27.

But what does a dynamic executive mean? Whatever it connotes, it must also be measured somehow by performance.

Four groups of chief operating officers of corporations, all of them in their present jobs for at least five years, were asked to take the tests. These men had held office long enough to assume responsibility for the reliability of their decisions and the recent performance of their companies.

The first two groups of chief executives were divided into two classes: those who had at least doubled profits in the past five years, and those who had not. The second group included some who had lost money.

Of the 12 men whose companies doubled their profits, 11 scored above the chance level on the computer guessing game. One scored at the chance level, and not a single one fell below chance.

Of the 13 who had not doubled profits, seven scored below chance, one scored at chance, and five scored above chance. This last five had improved profits by 50 to 100 percent. Of the seven who scored below chance, five had improved profits less than 50 percent. Only two of those who scored below chance had improved profits more substantially than that.

The chief executives who had more than doubled their companies' profits in five years had an average score of 12.8. Those who had not met this criteria scored an average of 8.3, well below what they should have achieved even on a random basis.

To give one striking example of the difference between the two groups: Over a five-year period, one president had increased his company's annual profit from $1.3 million to $19.4 million. His test score was 16. Another had been able to increase his profit by only $374,000. His score was eight.

The third group of participants consisted of 41 members of the Steel Distributors Association. Of the 41, 11 had been a company president for at least a five-year tenure. Of those 11, nine had at least doubled their company's profits over the last five years. Eight of these nine scored above chance. Their average was 11.44 percent. The remaining two, who had not at least doubled their company profits, averaged 9.5 percent, with both scoring at chance or less.

The fourth group was composed of 20 Canadian businesspeople. Of them, six had been company presidents in their current job for at least five years. Five of the six at least doubled the profits, while one fell into the 50 to 95 percent improvement class. Of the five profit-doublers, three scored above chance; the other two were below chance. The sixth person scored at chance level.

This finding has interesting implications for selection of executives for the "top spot." Given a group of people who have the usual traits needed for such a position, which one should be selected?

I feel that it should be the person with the something "extra"; in this case, the ability to make good decisions under conditions of uncertainty.

In the groups of company presidents tested, had the selection been made on the basis of their scores, there would have been an 81.5 percent chance of choosing a person who at least doubled the company's profits, while if someone who scored below chance had been chosen, there would have been only a 27.3 percent chance of choosing a person who would have doubled the company's profits.

DEVELOPMENT OF PRECOGNITION ABILITIES

Precognition is not a mystical origin, but rather an energy or information transfer using senses currently not recognizable or known. I believe that everyone has this ability. It is thus not a question of having precognitive ability, but rather one of developing the use of the precognitive ability we all possess.

Precognitive information comes in many forms—dreams at night, daydreams, flashes, hunches, and "gut feelings." The user has to first be aware of these various forms and then look for their appearance.

With precognition abilities, usage sharpens the talent.

With executives, it has been found that they believe in precognition, use it, and then build a rationale to justify the idea they used, or the decision they made, so as "to not look foolish."

Precognitive information is usually obtained concerning a matter in which the problem-solver has been deeply and emotionally involved. It also tends to arrive at times when the mind is supposedly resting and not thinking specifically about the problem.

Problem-solvers accept and use such information to make decisions, find solutions, and form ideas. There are many engineers and scientists, but the number of those who can come up with good ideas is very small.

These superior idea-generators review the same hard data that others have, but they must contribute something extra to come up with their ideas. Could not part of this something extra be their ability to gather information through what is loosely called ESP?

THE UTILIZATION OF PRECOGNITION ABILITY

Research on precognition ability does not support the idea that this ability is a unique trait. However, it does support the idea that some people have more of this ability—and make better use of it—than others.

The executive who wishes to avail himself of the ability to use precognition must first understand the nature and form of this phenomenon.

Precognition is a part of the unconscious process. As such, it is not bound by the usual limitations of space and time.

The ideal condition for the utilization of precognition information is when it does not require decoding or interpretation. The interpretation process, which tends to be logical and rational, can rework the illogical, but incorrect, information.

An example of getting precognition information would be the sudden thought that comes to an automobile driver to take a side road rather than the usual straight and shorter highway. The thought is not heeded, and later on down the highway, the motorist runs into a traffic jam.

Sir Winston Churchill is reported to have had "a feeling" that caused him to sit on the side of the car that he never uses. Later on during the auto trip, as the auto was speeding down the road, a bomb exploded, causing the auto to rise up on two side wheels. Due to Churchill's weight, the auto did not turn over but righted itself. Had Churchill not heeded the information that came to him, he would probably have been killed.

The executives studied not only had to be able to recognize the format of precognition information, but they also had to be prepared to get it any time. For them, this was not an ability that could be turned on and off at will.

Next, the user of precognition information has to have the faith and "guts" to use it. It is necessary to accept the existence of the phenomenon, whether or not the user knows how or why it happens.

Finally, the "practice makes perfect" rule should be followed. The intuitive decision-maker has to make using precognition information a habit.

Each decision-maker has to test the existence of precognition for himself with an open and positive mental attitude.

If you deny its existence, you are, in effect, repressing it, and it will go away. We tend, out of fear, to resist anything we do not understand. Our research indicates that the best results were achieved when resistance was at a minimum. For ESP abilities to function, we have to overcome any resistance we may have.

Several individuals I know had precognition abilities, were frightened of them, and ultimately managed to suppress them. When they realized that the ability could be very useful, a more relaxed attitude resulted and the ability began to return.

Common sense dictates that in any situation where knowledge is incomplete, the approach should be gentle. This is probably the best advice one can offer concerning precognition.

Be willing to believe that it exists. Have the courage to use it.

WHAT INHIBITS PRECOGNITION ABILITY

Do not expect to get good intuitive action under stressful conditions. When test subjects are under stress, the results follow the inverse hypothesis—that is, the dynamic managers who should have scored above chance did not do so. In fact, they scored below chance.

Similarly, you should not expect good results when you are tired or physically under par. Precognition tests consistently indicate that better results are achieved when tests are held early in the day.

Alcohol may also impair precognitive ability. After a three-martini lunch, dynamics from a group of production engineers scored 9.9 on average, and nondynamics scored 9.3 on average. The entire group, in other words, scored below chance. While we cannot with certainty blame the martinis, much evidence already exists concerning alcohol's effect on mental processes. I would suspect that ESP is no exception.

Lastly, you should probably try not to make intuitive decisions in any environment where you feel dominated. If you do, it is possible you may "intentionally" predict the future incorrectly.

It appears that if you are assured of a dominant role in the environment, and have precognitive ability, you will probably score high, almost as if validating the status quo. We call this the dominance effect.

But if your role is a dominated one, you may reinforce the existing hierarchical structure by "deliberately" scoring low.

During tests with mixed-sex groups, the dominating sex followed the hypothesis; dynamics scored higher than nondynamics. But the dominated sex produced a mirror image—that is, dynamics scored lower.

In another case, executives/owners who were fathers or fathers-in-law dominated their sons and sons-in-law. (By dominance we do not mean numerical superiority. It might better be termed environmental.)

In tests in groups where the environment was discernibly dominated by one sex, the dominance effect was noted. In groups where the sexes met on an equal footing, there was no mirror imaging or following of the inverse hypothesis.

USING PRECOGNITION FOR GOOD BUSINESS

Here is a story from Silva instructor Nelda Sheets about a time when she used precognition abilities to obtain information to help her employer make a major business decision, in her own words:

When you practice using your intuition enough, you learn to recognize that special feeling of being right. Jose Silva referred to this as an emotional feeling.

I was the office manager and a salesperson for a John Deere dealership. My boss and I had taken the Silva training together and used it for such things as mentally encouraging people to pay their bills. If we reached a certain sales quota, we'd win a trip to Nassau in the Bahamas. Our goal was 50 tractors.

When it was time to place our next order, my boss and I worked a case to determine what kind of tractors our customers would need. Normally I was the orientologist, but this time he was. I was the psychic. I went to level and asked how many diesel tractors we should order but was interrupted by a sign on my mental screen flashing the words "order all 50 tractors now" over and over. I told Gene, my boss, and he tried to talk me out of it. (We normally ordered five tractors at a time.) Gene had another concern: our bank balance.

I took a deep breath, relaxed, and did some deepening exercises to make sure I was at a good deep level. I mentally asked the question again. In response, I got the same neon sign flashing, telling me to order all 50 tractors. This time, I got that familiar feeling that I was right. I knew I was right, and I told Gene. Gene agreed this time, but because of a tax incentive he knew about. Having tractors in stock once a tax break was announced would help the business.

We ordered all 50 tractors. The John Deere people called me, thinking it was a mistake, since we always order just five at a time. The tractors were delivered, but our lot would only hold five! We had tractors parked in every empty space we could find. The local paper even came to do a story on us.

About a week later we got a call from the John Deere office saying that their workers had gone on strike and that no more equipment would be available. We had our tractors, and we sold all 50. And we enjoyed Nassau!

Professor Emeritus John Mihalasky, EdD, taught industrial engineering at The New Jersey Institute of Technology (formerly Newark College of Engineering) for 31 years. He was the director of the PSI Communications Project. After he retired in 1987, he continued to teach part-time. He is one of the authors of Executive ESP (Prentice Hall, 1974), the book about the landmark research project on precognition. He died in 2006 after a long and distinguished career.

Section VI: Success with ESP

Chapter 18
A Medical Breakthrough
by Prof. Clancy D. McKenzie, M.D.

In September 1969, I took my first Silva Mind Control class—spurred on by the guarantee of clairvoyance or a full money-back guarantee. The experience was exhilarating. No one asked for a refund, and skeptics like myself seemed particularly impressed.

The timing was just right. I had completed formal academic training, including adult and child psychiatry residency programs and adult and child psychoanalytic training courses. This left me free to study my patients and to apply methods of creative thinking as taught in the Silva course.

Looking back, I recognize five ingredients that were vital components for my discovery of new concepts in the field. For many years I recognized only the first four.

The first was the thorough background and formal training I received.

The second was a separation from that body of knowledge for a period of time. You cannot see a cloud when you are in it; you must first separate to catch its outline and see beyond.

The third was creative thinking, which Jose Silva taught me.

The fourth ingredient was love. All of my efforts at deciphering cause, mechanisms, and treatment for serious disorders were propelled strictly out of a sincere desire to help my patients. It is this propelling force that provides the energy, the clarity, and the insights for healing.

Jose Silva's course utilizes the same love energy for psychic diagnosis: Each trainee pictures the patient for the purpose of trying to help that individual, and according to Mr. Silva, it is largely because of this intended purpose that the trainee is able to do so much. As soon as the trainee begins thinking, *Look what I can do*, it is gone! It then is necessary to change that thinking to *let me find out what is wrong with this person and what I can do to help*. With that, the magic returns.

The creative techniques are taught well enough in the basic Silva course, and so there is no need to repeat them here—nor would this chapter allow enough space. Instead I will briefly summarize the findings for you.

The fifth ingredient is without doubt the most important of all; it is the higher guidance that orchestrates all that we do. Reflecting over the last 40 years, I see a long series of coincidences, synchronicities, visions, messages during the night, doors that were slammed shut, bigger doors that opened, each of which propelled me in the one direction— and without which nothing would have been accomplished.

THE MYSTERY SOLVED

Often what is most profound, once revealed, is profoundly simple. I hope this is your experience as you read these next few pages, within which I describe a new origin for schizophrenia, depression, and other serious disorders.

Everyone understands po-sttraumatic stress disorder caused by combat. A car backfires next to a combat veteran, and he grabs a gun and hides in the woods for a few days. His reality and behavior change to that of wartime; even his body chemistry and physiology match that of the earlier time when his life was in extreme danger.

We "understand" because the earlier events associated with loud noise were so life-threatening that they were indelibly etched upon his mind and brain.

What we fail to recognize is that more terrifying than war trauma to a soldier is separation from the mother to an infant. To all mammalian infants, for as long as they have populated the earth, separation from mother has meant death. Thus the human infant is highly susceptible to what *it* considers to be a threat of separation.

This need not be an obvious threat of separation, such as one caused by the death of a parent or by parental divorce. Unsuspected events can overwhelm the infant and set the stage for the later development of a serious disorder. Such traumas might include the family moving to a new house and the mother busying herself making the new place look like home, or an older child becoming deathly ill and requiring all the mother's attention for a period of time. In pervious generations, the birth of a younger sibling was devastating because mothers spent five days in the hospital following delivery. These separations might not seem traumatic from the adult perspective, but from an infant's point of view they can be overwhelming. Any event that results in the mother's temporary absence or distraction, potentially, can frighten the infant very much and leave the indelible mark etched upon its mind and brain.

Then 10, 20, or 30 years later, instead of a loud noise precipitating the flashback, it is a separation from some other "most important person" (husband, wife, girlfriend, boyfriend, or group) that precipitates the initial step back in time. And instead of combat reality and behavior, it is infant reality and behavior that we see. A full-grown man, for example, might sit in the middle of the floor, screaming, "Mommy! Mommy!"

The first time I witnessed this I was only 5 years old. An 18-year-old girl was running nude through the lawn sprinkler in the front yard, squealing with delight. As a young child I thought, *What's wrong with her? Grown-ups don't do that.*

It took a quarter of a century for me to realize that this was perfectly normal behavior, but transposed in time. Had she been 18 *months* old instead of 18 years old, no one would have thought anything odd about her behavior.

With careful examination, virtually every piece of bizarre reality and behavior of the person with schizophrenia matches in some way that of the infant, and when you have studied this as carefully, and for as long as I have, you will realize that it matches the reality and behavior of the infant at the *precise time* or age that the original trauma occurred.

Simple so far? Just like post-traumatic stress disorder from combat where a loud noise 20 years after the original trauma precipitates a flashback to war experience and behavior because loud noise was associated with terrifying experiences of war, a separation from a "most important person" 20 years after the original trauma precipitates the flashback to the infant experience and behavior because the infant feared separation and felt equally overwhelmed.

THE DIFFERENCE

The most important difference between the combat veteran and the person with schizophrenia is that while the veteran flashes back to the brain structures he was using as an adult, the person with schizophrenia flashes back to the brain structures he was using as an infant.

These are the earlier developmental regions of the brain, the parts of the brain we were using at the precise time of the original trauma, before we learned to walk or talk.

These earlier developmental structures are the ones that produce more of the neurotransmitters involved in the disease process, such as dopamine, and when they are reactivated, they produce more! Is this not obvious? Why has no one suspected this? Why has everyone looked only from the opposite direction and wondered how dopamine causes schizophrenia?

Likewise there is a corresponding shift of brain activity away from the later developmental structures. Remember the grown man sitting in the middle of the floor screaming for his mommy? Was he using the part of his brain that developed in adult life? Obviously not. And what happens to a part of the body that becomes less active? It *atrophies*. This is much like the common expression "use it or lose it." So the brain atrophies as the result of the disease process.

Aside from the search for a biological cause, there is yet another area of investigation that continues to take center stage over and over again: the search for genetic cause. In reality, only about one in 10 schizophrenics has a first-degree relative with the disorder—and half or more of them more likely are familial (habitual) instead of hereditary!

Contrast that with the ratio between delayed post-traumatic stress disorder from infancy (schizophrenia) and original trauma. This is a one-to-one ratio, because we cannot have delayed post-traumatic stress disorder without original trauma.

So why hasn't anyone thought that schizophrenia causes an increase in dopamine and causes brain atrophy? Why do researchers only look at brain changes and wonder how these cause schizophrenia?

The answer might lie in motives for the search. Jesus said we could not serve two masters. Drug companies search for cause as long as it relates to something they can sell. The National Institute of Mental Health (NIMH) searches for cause as long as it is biological, because Congress allocates 1.3 billions each year to search for biological cause. The National Alliance for the Mentally Ill (NAMI), hurting from unfair blame, searches for cause as long as God did it, because if it is not an act of God, family members might feel worse than they already do. (My heart really goes out to them because they suffer enormously, and they truly are not to blame.)

So the big three, searching for cause, have eliminated cause from the search!

Isaiah 44:25: Thus says the Lord: *I am the Lord that turns wise men backward and makes their knowledge foolish.* Could this be what is happening? It looks like it to me!

THE UNIFICATION THEORY OF MENTAL ILLNESS

What we have been describing thus far is a comprehensive formulation for the origin and mechanism of schizophrenia. It is a *delayed* post-traumatic stress disorder mechanism that applies to all serious mental and emotional disorders that I have studied, and for which the noted late Dr. O. Spurgeon English coined the name, the Unification Theory of Mental Illness.

The Unification model neither refutes biological change nor precludes genetic predisposition. I have no quarrel with any biological finding. The researchers have done their jobs very well. And their findings are important, because just as a chain can be broken at any link, so can schizophrenia be interrupted at many levels. Biological findings also confirm psychological origin, because nearly every biological change studied is precisely what we should expect to find when persons shift brain activity away from adult brain structures and back to regions of the brain that were active and developing during infancy.

Genetic factors represent predisposition, and their degree of contribution is not yet determined to my satisfaction. This does not change traumatic origin. Schizophrenia has a one to one correlation with early trauma, because delayed post-traumatic stress disorder cannot occur without earlier trauma.

This is a *delayed* post-traumatic stress disorder mechanism. Persons continue to have flashbacks, nightmares, and intrusive thoughts, which accumulate in the age-of-origin-specific mind and brain. If the trauma occurs at age 1 year, then it becomes like a growing abscess of troubled thoughts in the 1-year-old mind. With each flashback, nightmare, and intrusive thought, there is an enormous process of repression that occurs. This serves as the wall of the abscess, which protects the individual from the painful thoughts within. As this abscess of the mind grows, the defensive wall thickens. Eventually, 10, 20, or 30 years later, there is a symptom-precipitating trauma that is sufficiently intense and similar to the original symptom-defining trauma that it breaks through the defensive wall, stirs this abscess of the mind, and causes a volcanic eruption and surfacing of the unconscious material that has been repressed over the years.

This surfaces as the acute positive symptoms of schizophrenia. The massive defensive wall of repression is recognized as the precursors of schizophrenia (the child is shy, timid, does not socialize or participate in rough sports—and does nothing to stir the sleeping giant in the unconscious mind). After the appearance of the acute positive symptoms, this same defensive wall changes names and now is called the negative symptoms of schizophrenia.

This same mechanism operates in all delayed post-traumatic stress disorders from any age, and it has the same components and the same derivation. In fact, all these disorders meet criteria for delayed post-traumatic stress disorder. The major difference is that following the volcanic eruption of the repressed material, the defensive wall no longer is as intact, and recurrences happen with little further provocation. Thus, following an initial psychosis there are recurrent psychotic episodes; following major depression there are recurrent major depressive episodes; following an initial panic, phobic, or anxiety attack there are recurrences of the same; and following the initial "crossing the invisible line" in alcoholism, all it requires is one drink to start the process all over again.

Why has no one seen any of these things? They are so simple I can explain them to a young child, yet the entire mental health community continues to look in the wrong direction for cause.

Autism and symbiosis represent acute instead of delayed post-traumatic stress disorders. With the 20-fold increase in autism, why has no one conducted a simple survey of the incidence among offspring of working versus nonworking mothers? Separation is the most overwhelming trauma to infants, and the 20-fold increase coincides with the advent of the working mother.

SUMMARY

You now have an overview of the origin of schizophrenia and other serious disorders. There might or might not be significant genetic predisposition. Regardless of this factor, in order to develop the disorder later in life, there must be an infant separation trauma. I have not seen this to be otherwise, whenever the history is known. There are thousands of events that can cause the infant to feel threatened with separation and overwhelmed, and most of these are not obvious to the adult. This is no one's fault, and the events are unintentional.

Many years later, a spouse, friend, or group rejects or leaves the person. If this experience is sufficiently intense and similar to the first, then the individual can flash back to the time of the original trauma, and exhibit the infant reality, behavior, and feelings. The person also shifts brain activity to earlier developmental regions, which results in the biological change.

This is the essence of the Unification Theory of Mental Illness, and if you understand this much, then in my opinion you understand more than most physicians, more than most researchers, and more than the National Institute of Mental Health. You certainly do not know more *about* the disorder, but you have a better understanding of its origin and how it works. This is very important, because with this understanding you will be able to understand prevention, and why it is unnecessary to have the disorder.

Lastly, in reviewing how the above information was gathered over the years, I am amazed at what I myself never had recognized until recently. The development of intuitive techniques, combined with the sincere desire to help the 45 million families around the world who suffer unnecessarily with schizophrenia, the five times as many with depression, and more with bipolar disorder, ADHD, school violence, autism, symbiosis, borderline personality disorder, alcohol and drug dependence, eating disorders, and more, brought help from a higher source.

As I reflect over the last four decades, I realize that the information came through dreams, visions, coincidences, synchronicities, messages during the night, visits from angels during the night, strange occurrences, one door slamming shut and another opening—without which I could not have continued on the journey. Even my interests and hobbies, from early childhood, seemed to be preparing me precisely for this journey.

All this came from higher up. I can't claim credit for any of it. I had a desire to help, so much of a desire that I was even working on the problems at night, programming for dreams to provide guidance. It was dreams, visions, coincidences, synchronicities, and so on, that guided me to these conclusions. I take no credit for myself—other than being an unsuspecting messenger. To God be the glory for the work He has done!

Note from Ed Bernd Jr.: Such insights, those that change an entire field of thought, come only through enlightenment techniques. (Dr. McKenzie credits the Silva training with introducing him to techniques that started him on a journey inward and allowed for intuitive answers.) With the help of the creative insights that he gained at the alpha level, Dr. McKenzie made a major medical breakthrough in understanding the cause of schizophrenia and depression. His findings as to origin have been tested and confirmed on 9,000 patients with schizophrenia, and his treatment methods, based on that insight, are so effective that many patients no longer need medication after the first few months. More of Dr. McKenzie's work, including his new treatment methods and his textbook, are featured on www.DrMcKenzie.com.

This chapter is copyright of the American Mental Health Association.

Chapter 19
Using Everyday ESP

Even though my father had not originally started his research in order to train people to be psychic, he did not call it an accident. He often said that he was guided by higher intelligence to make the discoveries that he made.

After he realized that he could train anybody to be a psychic, he began to think about all of the ways that this ability could be of value. Silva graduates have used psychic ability in a wide variety of fields over the years. This chapter includes a few of my favorites.

POLICE OFFICERS PROJECT CALM IN TENSE SITUATIONS

Silva graduate Denis McKeon, a retired police officer from New Orleans, Louisiana, used mental projection to help him deal with violent hostility. The Silva System seemed to hold hope, so he repeated the program, seeking techniques to help him achieve his goal. He found a technique for dealing with confrontations that he considers ideal. Here's his story, in his own words:

> I wanted to find a way to prevent crime and violence instead of constantly dealing with the aftermath of these incidents.
>
> When an individual or a small group of people confront you and are angry or projecting hatred and insults, remain calm. When they insult you, just smile and say, "Thank you." This will surprise them.
>
> While they are confused, mentally project love, peace, and brotherhood toward them. The majority of the time this tactic will break the

tension and either end the situation or allow you to deal with these people in a rational way. This will eliminate the possibility of violence.

I discovered this method when I was confronted by an individual who was very angry, calling me vile names and threatening violence.

I remembered the beneficial statement that "Negative thoughts and actions will have no influence over me at any level of the mind." I decided to try to avoid violence by using positive mental projection, but first I had to stop his advance.

I smiled and said, "Thank you. That's the nicest thing anyone has said to me today." This stopped him in his tracks with a bewildered look on his face. This gave me the few seconds I needed to mentally project love, peace, and brotherhood toward him.

The result was that he slowly started to smile and he said, "You know, you're okay," and then he wanted to shake my hand. The potential for a violent situation had passed.

By using the method I have described, violence may be avoided most of the time. I found this technique to be effective in about 80 percent of these types of confrontations.

One other technique he has used involves mental projection at a distance.

McKeon said that he would mentally project to every area of his post each day before he started his rounds. He would visualize everything peaceful and harmonious. Here's how he explains it:

After I had been using this technique for a while, I started to observe that the residents of my post were beginning to act less fearful, there was much less anxiety present, and the people were happier in general.

Their attitude toward me changed also. They became very friendly toward me and were always glad to see me. They gave me the nickname of "Smiley, the happy cop." This did wonders for me also. At the end of my day I felt a sense of accomplishment and satisfaction, whereas before, I had felt frustrated and depressed.

I know this method works. I have used it successfully for many years. At the same time, the surrounding posts had all kinds of problems.

PSYCHIC ABILITY AIDS ATTORNEYS

Marcelino Alcala has been a Silva instructor in the Caribbean for more than 20 years. He is also an attorney, and he reports that psychic ability has helped him in many ways.

Lawyers usually prefer to reach a settlement rather than deal with the uncertainty of a trial. Marcelino uses the creative insights and information of the alpha level to help him come up with ways to settle cases that are acceptable to all parties. This is exactly like one of the affirmations that my father included in the Silva UltraMind System: "The solution must be the best for all concerned."

Diana Navarro, an attorney in Laredo, Texas, said that a client of hers was trying to negotiate an agreement but ran into trouble. Acting on a verbal agreement, her client invested money in a project. After he made the investment, the supposed partner wanted to add several conditions to the verbal agreement they had previously made.

"They were not making any progress," Diana said, "and my client was getting very frustrated. I told him I'd see what I could do to help."

The next day the client called to say that everything was resolved. "All I had done the night before," Diana said, "was to enter my level, visualize the parties to the agreement—I knew both of them—and program that the other person would tell my client what it was that he *really* wanted. And that's exactly what he did the next morning."

There are no secrets at alpha. Psychics can detect the truth, no matter how hard you try to conceal it. Marcelino said that's been a big help to him when he is cross-examining witnesses. "When you can sense that a witness is lying, then you know what areas to delve into," he explained.

A PILOT SEES INTO THE FUTURE

In 1986 a woman named Tweet Coleman joined us in Amarillo, Texas, to celebrate the 20th anniversary of the first commercial Silva class. A year earlier, Tweet had gotten a job as a pilot for a major airline.

When flying, she uses her mind to check for problems. Here is Tweet's story, in her own words:

> Sometimes when you're flying you will hear things in the airplane, or the flight attendants will come up and they will hear things, and you have to go back and check it out.
>
> A couple of weeks ago, a flight attendant told us that on takeoff it appeared that the hubcap on the right tire was making a noise.
>
> I went to level and I mentally pictured the tire and the mechanism around the tire. Plane tires don't have hubcaps, but something else could have been wrong.

I sensed that two of the four cotter pins around the wheel were missing. There was nothing I could do in the air, so I went ahead to our destination. On landing, the flight attendant reported the same situation again. After the flight, a mechanic and I checked, and, sure enough, the cotter pins had fallen out.

Another way psychic ability helps me is with the weather. We have radar in the airplanes, and it is about 95 percent reliable. Sometimes there are problems. An airplane pilot needs to know whether to go left or right, up or down.

You need to use your intuition and your radar. I think they are about equal in importance. So I have used it a lot of times to see through the clouds and see through the weather to make the right decision. That's really helped a lot.

I fly from Guam to Japan, Manilla, and so on. You are not always in radar control. It is not like on the mainland where you are always talking to somebody. You make a report about every 30 minutes, but other than that, you are not talking to anybody.

So if you see some weather in front of you, it is up to you to determine what to do. By visualizing the weather, picturing the movement of the weather, then you can make right or left turns as necessary. This is pretty exciting.

The International Society of Women Airline Pilots lists Tweet Coleman as a member of the first all-female B727 flight crew in the world.

Tweet believes in doing something for those who will follow in her footsteps. She has established the Tweet Coleman Aviation Scholarship through the American Association of University Women. This provides several thousands of dollars in scholarships each year to young women who want to pursue careers as active cockpit crew members.

Tweet credits the Silva techniques, which she learned in the 1970s, with helping her to achieve so much success. And she has certainly taken my father's guidance to heart: to leave behind a better world for those who follow.

Appendix

Resources

Information about Silva Courses and products

www.SilvaCourses.com.

To contact the authors of this book or any Silva instructor, and for a schedule of Silva seminars, please visit the Silva Instructors Website.

www.SilvaInstructors.com.

Silva Alumni Association Website

www.Silva.SupportGroup.ws

Silva books, recordings, home-study courses

www.SilvaShop.com

Ecumenical Society Holistic Faith Healing Website

www.ESPsy.org

If you have a health problem and want Silva graduates to program for you, or if you are a Silva graduate and want health cases to work, please visit this Website.

www.HealthCases.com

Jose Silva Jr.'s Website

www.JRSystemsManagement.com

Ed Bernd Jr. works with Avlis Publishing and Avlis Productions Inc.

www.AvlisPub.com

Dr. Clancy McKenzie

www.DrMcKenzie.com

Cleve Backster

www.primaryperception.com

Dr. Bruce Lipton
 www.brucelipton.com
Silva UltraMind Website
 www.UltraMind.ws
Silva International Inc. Website
 www.silvamethod.com
More information about Jose Silva's Everyday ESP
 www.EverydayESP.com
New Page Books
 www.newpagebooks.com

Index

About the Authors

JOSE SILVA JR.

Jose Silva Jr. (known as Joe or Joe Jr. to his friends) is one of the last links to his father's pioneering research that led to the development of a system to help everyone develop their natural God-given ESP, so they can use it and benefit from it every day, in every area of life.

Joe was born in 1941, the first of Jose and Paula Silva's 10 children. When his father began to experiment with hypnosis in the late 1940s, using Joe's younger sisters and brothers as subjects, Joe was there to help and to document much of the research. He recorded prenatal age regression sessions when his siblings went back to so-called "past life regressions."

Joe was in the U.S. Navy serving in Vietnam when his father began taking his findings to the public via a series of workshops in the mid 1960s. There was a huge demand for Jose Silva's "Mind Control" system, as it was called it back then, so in 1967 Mr. Silva asked Joe to come back to Laredo as soon as he could to help take care of the electronics repair business.

When the new seminar business began to grow, Joe helped manage it too, and was one of the three incorporators of Silva International, the corporation that still manages the original course.

In 1995, Mr. Silva nominated Joe to take over the presidency of Silva International, a position he has held ever since. In 1998, when they set up a separate company to manage the new Silva UltraMind ESP System, Joe was named president of that company and assigned the majority ownership.

Throughout the tremendous growth of the Silva programs from their modest beginnings in Laredo, Texas, to more than 100 nations around the world, Joe has been the most consistent factor, along with his father and his Uncle Juan, who both passed on in 1999.

Joe has been married to his wife, Ruth, since 1967. They have two children, David and Ruthie, and five grandchildren. Joe holds a black belt in karate, and served as a consultant to Ed Bernd Jr. in developing the Silva Star Athlete program and *The Silva Method—Think and Grow Fit* book (published by Career Press in 1996).

ED BERND JR.

Ed Bernd Jr. grew up in the newspaper business and said he was way beyond skeptical about ESP—he was certain that it didn't exist. He took the course to learn more about how the brain works, hoping that this would help him in his weightlifting hobby. He fully intended to ask for a refund at the completion of the seminar.

Much to his surprise, after two weekends of mental training exercises Ed was functioning as a psychic with about 80 percent accuracy. So were the other 150 people in the class. So instead of asking for a refund, he wound up leaving the newspaper business and becoming a Silva instructor.

Ed says that he has used his ESP virtually every day since he attended that first Silva program back in 1975. He became a Silva instructor in 1977, and was invited to join the Silva world headquarters staff in 1981 as an instructor and editor of the company newsletter. He quickly began putting his communications skills to work to let people know about the benefits of the program.

He worked for Jose Silva for the last 17 years of Mr. Silva's life. In addition to lecturing, he also managed the Silva alumni association, developed specialized programs for athletes and salespeople under Mr. Silva's guidance, and worked with Mr. Silva on more than a dozen books as editor or coauthor. He is the coauthor of Jose Silva's last four books.

Ed and Joe Jr. are the same age (Ed is five months older) and they have been close friends ever since they met when Ed came to Laredo for instructor training for the first time in 1977. "The day I came to work here at headquarters in 1981," Ed recalled, "Joe told me that I wouldn't be treated like an employee, that they treat everybody like family. It has been a wonderful adventure and an honor to have been associated with them for all these years."